FOR ALL
THOSE MEN

ISBN 13 (paper): 978-1-946160-90-4

http://ulpress.org
University of Louisiana at Lafayette Press
P.O. Box 43558
Lafayette, LA 70504-3558

Printed in the United States

Library of Congress Cataloging-in-Publication Data

Names: Smith, John Warner, 1952- author.
Title: For all those men : when the KKK threatened to take control of
    Louisiana / John Warner Smith.
Description: Lafayette : University of Louisiana at Lafayette Press, 2022.
Identifiers: LCCN 2022022502 | ISBN 9781946160904 (paperback)
Subjects: LCSH: Hebert, Emile,--Trials, litigation, etc. | Trials
    (Murder)--Louisiana. | Trials (Assault and battery)--Louisiana. |
    African Americans--Louisiana--History--20th century. | Louisiana--
Race
    relations--20th century. | Ku Klux Klan (1915-) | Reconstruction (U.S.
    history, 1865-1877) | Parker, John Milliken, 1863-1939
Classification: LCC KF224.H425 S65 2022 | DDC
    345.763/025--dc23/eng/20220801
LC record available at https://lccn.loc.gov/2022022502

Grateful acknowledgment to:
Dennis Paul Williams for cover art
Philip Gould for cover art photography

FOR ALL THOSE MEN

When the KKK Threatened to Take Control of Louisiana

JOHN WARNER SMITH

UNIVERSITY OF LOUISIANA AT LAFAYETTE PRESS
2022

For the family of Emile Hebert

INTRODUCTION

In 1922, Louisiana stood on the edge of a precipice. Racial turmoil divided the state. The Ku Klux Klan had not only infiltrated north Louisiana, its membership had grown substantially, to the point that, through the elected and appointed officials who had joined its ranks, the Klan controlled the entire northern half of the state. They had also established chapters in the predominantly Catholic south-central and southwest parishes. Louisiana Governor John M. Parker's concern—not unfounded—was that, if unchecked, the Klan's domination would eventually blanket the entire state.

That summer, two tragic events occurred, one in the north, another in the south, that dramatically changed the state's racial and political climate. In the south, a tragic shooting in Lafayette Parish involved Emile Hebert, a young, Black farmer, and four white men. The shooting resulted in the death of a prominent resident of Rayne, Louisiana, and the serious injury of the sheriff of Lafayette Parish. Hebert's murder trial was set to begin in October. On rumors that a mob of men, led by the KKK, were plotting to seize the prisoner and hang him, Governor Parker deployed the National Guard to protect the courthouse, marking the first time in parish history that the military was used in connection with a trial.

Two months before the start of Hebert's trial, two white men, Filmore Watt Daniel and Thomas F. Richards (both of whom had reportedly spoken out against the KKK), mysteriously disappeared in the plantation village of Mer Rouge, located in Morehouse Parish. The men were found dead four months later. Governor Parker, halfway into his four-year term, became intensely involved in the Mer Rouge case. The murders gained national attention and are largely credited with ending the stronghold of the Ku Klux Klan in north Louisiana and contributing to the decline of its influence nationally.

The trial of Emile Hebert remains a relatively obscure event in the annals of Lafayette Parish judicial history and Louisiana political history. As told here, Hebert's court case takes center stage, as does Governor Parker and the role he played in stopping the KKK's rise to power. Court transcriptions of the trial of Hebert were lost in a fire decades ago. This story recreates history. Although the dialogue is fictional, the story is based on real people and real events, reconstructed here, one hundred years later, as accurately as possible based on newspaper articles, court records, internet sources, and information provided by members of the Hebert family. In some instances, when facts about real people or events were not known or could not be confirmed, details were omitted.

To fully grasp the historical significance and impact of the Mer Rouge murders and the Hebert case, one must trace the racial and political turmoil that occurred in the South during the nearly six decades preceding Louisiana's "red summer" of 1922.

Immediately after the Civil War ended in 1865, the defeated Confederate states enacted restrictive laws, commonly called "Black Codes," to limit the freedom of former slaves. In response, the federal government placed southern states under military rule and passed legislation to protect the citizenship and basic rights of African Americans, setting in motion a twelve-year period known as the Reconstruction era. From 1865 to 1877, federal laws were passed to rebuild a divided nation and grant equal protection and civil rights to Black citizens. Among the federal actions taken was the establishment of the Bureau of Refugees, Freedmen, and Abandoned Lands (commonly known as the Freedmen's Bureau) in 1865, which gave relief aid to African Americans. Through the bureau, thousands of northerners traveled to the South to set up schools, establish cooperatives, and provide skills training to freed Black men and women. Between 1866 and 1868, historically Black colleges such as Fisk, Morehouse, Howard, Atlanta, Talladega, and Hampton were established. The most significant Reconstruction legislation were three Constitutional amendments passed by the Republican-controlled US government. Enacted in 1865, the Thirteenth Amendment outlawed slavery. In 1868, the Fourteenth Amendment granted citizenship to all people born in the United States and provided equal protection under the law to all citizens (including Black people), and in 1870, the Fifteenth Amendment ensured that the right of citizens to vote could not be denied based on race.

In 1868, Louisiana adopted a constitution that was considered one of the most progressive in the United States. The constitution extended voting and other civil rights to Black men, established an integrated, free public school system, and guaranteed African American citizens equal access to public accommodations. In the election held in April of that year, Black men won forty-two of the 120 seats of the state legislature. Also in 1868, Louisiana elected an African American state treasurer, and Oscar Dunn was elected the state's first Black lieutenant governor, making him one of the first Black men to serve in an executive political position in the United States. When Dunn died in 1871, he was succeeded by P. B. S. Pinchback, a Black state senator who had become senate pro tempore. In December 1872, following the impeachment of Governor Henry Clay Warmoth on charges of using his political influence to falsify returns of the gubernatorial election of 1872, Pinchback was sworn in as acting governor, serving for thirty-six days, with the distinction of being the only African American to serve as governor of a southern state during Reconstruction.

After the state election of 1868, in which Republicans handily won local and state offices and many African Americans were elected, tension grew between Black voters and white Democrats, who opposed voting and civil rights for formerly enslaved people. Eventually, the tension escalated to violence and bloodshed. In St. Landry Parish, it reached a boiling point in the fall of 1868, in what became the deadliest massacre of the Reconstruction era in Louisiana. In the months leading up to the bloodshed, Emerson Bentley, an eighteen-year-old white schoolteacher for African American children and an editor for the *St. Landry Progress*, a local Republican newspaper, had been beaten for supposedly misrepresenting the Democratic Party in an article published in the journal. Rumors falsely spread that Bentley had been killed. Word also spread that Black people were organizing to take up arms in response to the treatment of Bentley. In September, thousands of white men, acting in fear of a rebellion by Black residents, armed themselves and started raiding homes. In a shocking display of white supremacist violence, white vigilante groups slaughtered as many as 250 residents of the parish over two weeks. Most of the victims were African American.

One month later, in St. Bernard Parish, just weeks before a presidential election that would decide the fate of Reconstruction in the South, a large but undetermined number of Black residents were killed by white protestors seeking to suppress the African American vote and end Reconstruction.

The fight over the post-Civil War government continued during and after the 1872 state election. On April 13, 1873, in Colfax, Louisiana, a confrontation between an all-Black armed group and several white protesters ended in a bloody battle at the site of the Grant Parish courthouse. The African American group had taken control of the courthouse in fear that Democrats would lead a coup of the local government. When white resistance forces arrived, a gun battle ensued, ending in the surrender of the Black militia and the subsequent killing of many of them. It is estimated that between sixty and 150 African Americans were killed, along with three white men.

A year later, the paramilitary White League was formed with the objective of overthrowing the Republican government in Louisiana. Founded in Grant Parish and aligned with the Democratic Party, the White League eventually reached New Orleans, where it saw its largest membership, and where, on September 14, 1874, the Battle of Liberty Place occurred. In that confrontation, thousands of men fought each other for the soul of their state government in the streets of New Orleans. More than thirty people died.

The violence that erupted, as white Democrats reacted to the loss of political power during Reconstruction, proved to be only a backdrop to the forces that would ultimately bring an end to Reconstruction. It began with machinations in national politics. In what is now known as the Compromise of 1877, the political backers of Rutherford B. Hayes, the Republican candidate for president, and moderate southern Democrats in Florida, Louisiana, and South Carolina struck a deal in a dispute over election returns of the US presidential election. The Democrats agreed not to contest Hayes's election in exchange for the Republicans' withdrawal of federal troops from the South. Without the enforcement of federal laws that had granted civil rights to African American people, southern states enacted what became known as "Jim Crow" laws to maintain racial segregation and white supremacy. As a result, most, if not all, of the political and social gains that freed Black people had made during Reconstruction were reversed.

Electoral disenfranchisement was particularly evident in Louisiana, the state that set the stage for the legal doctrine of "separate but equal" in the 1896 US Supreme Court decision of *Plessy v. Ferguson*. In 1898, three decades after the adoption of a state constitution that granted civil and voting rights to Black Louisianans and resulted in their making significant political gains in the legislature and statewide offices, Louisiana adopted a new constitution that stripped people of color of all political influence. As a result, the number of African American voters in Louisiana fell from 130,444 to 5,320. Due to a poll tax and other restrictions instituted by the new constitution, that number fell to 1,324 by 1904.

After *Plessy* and the enactment of the new constitution, Louisiana communities grew more racially segregated, socially and economically. In addition to suppressing the voting rights of Black people, the constitution required separate schools for white and Black students. In Lafayette Parish, there was not a single public high school for African Americans in 1922. At the turn of the twentieth century, most African Americans in Lafayette Parish were poor, working as laborers, domestic workers, and in other menial occupations. Within the corporate limits of Lafayette, colored people were restricted to housing within Black neighborhoods. For many African American residents of the parish, farming was the only way of life.

Violence against Blacks in Louisiana rose sharply during the post-Reconstruction era. Lynching claimed at least 355 African American lives between 1882 and 1952. Historian Adam Fairclough noted that between 1889 and 1922, the overwhelmingly Protestant parishes of north Louisiana, namely Caddo, Ouachita, and Morehouse, "witnessed more lynchings than any other counties in the nation."[1]

In the south-central parishes where sugarcane was the primary crop, white planters used intimidation tactics through the courts, and in some cases mob violence, to assert their power and influence as the upper rung of the caste system. In what is recognized as the second bloodiest labor dispute in US history, the Thibodaux Massacre of November 1887 resulted in the killing of between thirty-five and fifty Black residents.

It began when African American sugarcane workers had organized to protest low wages and how they were paid. Plantation owners paid the workers in coins or scrip that could only be redeemed at the plantation store, putting the workers at the mercy of the owners for the price of purchased goods. If the worker was indebted to the store, he was required by law to work on the plantation until the debt was paid, thus keeping freed workers in a system of continued enslavement. On November 1, 1887, at the peak of harvest time, an estimated ten thousand sugar plantation workers went on a strike that affected the region of Lafourche, Terrebonne, St. Mary, and Iberia parishes. On the morning of November 22nd, armed white men closed the entrances to Thibodaux. When two white men were fired upon, violence erupted. African American strikers and their families were

---

1. Adam Fairclough, *Race & Democracy: The Civil Rights Struggle in Louisiana, 1915–1972* (Athens: University of Georgia Press, 1995), 6–9.

rounded up and shot. By the turn of the century, the massacre still loomed as a reminder that in the southern parishes, sugar was king.

Much of the post-Civil War racial violence is attributable to the founding of the Ku Klux Klan. The KKK formed with the objective of reversing Reconstruction and restoring the enslavement of African Americans. Its tactics, carried out mostly at night, included lynching, torture, and terrorist acts directed at Blacks as well as whites who supported or sympathized with Reconstruction policies. The organization grew its membership largely in the South. With the aid of state laws that stripped away the political and economic advancements that African Americans had made during Reconstruction, the KKK achieved its aim of maintaining white supremacy through the political disenfranchisement and economic subjugation of African Americans.

According to historian Linda Gordon, the early 1920s marked "the second coming of the Ku Klux Klan," a period in which the organization rebranded its image, shifted its focus geographically and strategically, and expanded its constituency into mainstream America.[2] Unlike its predecessor, the second KKK concentrated its efforts largely in the North, where African Americans were fewer in number. The second Klan expanded by adding Catholics, Jews, immigrants, and bootleggers to its list of enemies and opposed prostitution. While the first KKK was mostly clandestine, the second Klan was much more open, holding mass public events, publishing recruitment ads in newspapers, and electing hundreds of members to political office. Gordon asserts that this KKK was supported by millions of Americans, perhaps even a majority, many of whom were not members of the Klan but who embraced the organization's philosophy of exclusion with the hope of greater social and economic status.[3]

Yet, as Fairclough contends, this was not the case for many whites in south Louisiana, largely due to the bitter opposition of Louisiana Catholics to the KKK when they entered the state in the early 1920s.[4] As a result, the second Klan did not attain the degree of political influence in Louisiana that it achieved in other states. Despite this, white supremacy reigned in the region, and, by 1922, the second KKK was a force to be reckoned with.

2. Linda Gordon, *The Second Coming of the KKK: The Ku Klux Klan of the 1920s and the American Political Tradition* (New York: Liveright Publishing Corporation, 2017), 1–26.
3. Gordon, *The Second Coming of the KKK*, 3.
4. Fairclough, *Race & Democracy*, 6–9.

———

In the early 1900s, sympathy for the Confederate states that had lost the Civil War had grown widespread throughout the South. People began to speak of the defeat of the South as the so-called "Lost Cause," celebrating the fallen Confederate soldiers as heroes fighting for a bygone era and protectors of states' rights. In one of hundreds of similar acts across the former Confederate states, on April 8, 1922, local elected officials of Lafayette Parish joined a former leader of the United Daughters of the Confederacy and Louisiana Governor John M. Parker to commemorate the unveiling of a monument of General Alfred Mouton. The monument was erected on city-owned land (which, in 1939, became the site of Lafayette's second city hall). At the time the monument was erected, the all-white Southside Primary School, Lafayette's first high school, stood on the opposite end of the block.[5]

General Mouton, the oldest son of former Louisiana Governor Alexandre Mouton, was trained at West Point Military Academy. Prior to becoming a commissioned officer in the Confederate army, he led a group that terrorized Black and white citizens under the guise of fighting crime and immorality. Inscribed on the pedestal of the twenty-one-foot-high monument, with a life-size replica of Mouton carved from Italian marble, are words recounting the general's distinguished military career. The monument was unveiled to commemorate the day in 1864 when the thirty-five-year-old general was killed in the Battle of Mansfield.[6]

5. The school closed long after the monument was built.
6. Nearly a century later, on July 16, 2021—in the culmination of a legal battle that dated back to 1980—the United Daughters of the Confederacy signed a settlement with the City of Lafayette agreeing to the monument's removal. Opponents of the monument, led by the local activist group Free the Mindset, and with the support of Lafayette Mayor-President Josh Guillory, argued that the stone replica of the bearded general, decked in military regalia and standing confidently with arms folded, had been erected in the middle of the downtown square in defense of the "Lost Cause" and as a declaration of the reign of white supremacy more than a half-century after the end of the Civil War and a quarter of a century after *Plessy v. Ferguson*. After standing for nearly one hundred years, this highly visible symbol of efforts to terrorize and dehumanize African Americans in post-Reconstruction Louisiana has been removed, but like other events of the second coming of the KKK, the erection of the Mouton monument remains a part of Louisiana's shameful history of racial hatred.

Ironically, the land on which the Mouton monument was erected had been sold to the City of Lafayette on February 16, 1921, for a price of $817 by the heirs of Archille Figaro, a Black man.[7] His father was Jean Figaro, an enslaved man who had been stolen from Africa at the age of sixteen. According to family sources, Alexandre Mouton was Jean Figaro's slaveholder. Archille Figaro had purchased the land from Alexandre Mouton on December 3, 1870, at the height of Reconstruction, for a price of $200, "payable one-half in one year and the other half in two years."[8]

One can assume that the Figaro heirs who inherited the land and sold it for public use had no idea that the property would one day be the site of a monument to a general who fought and died to defend the Confederacy and keep Black people enslaved, a general whose ancestors enslaved African American people and committed violence against their own.[9]

———

Such was the racial climate of Louisiana in 1922. It was a state divided, not only between north and south, but between those who clung to white supremacy, the vestiges of slavery and antebellum life, and those who still struggled to free themselves of it.

It should be noted that in the chapters of this book that follow, in which the events leading up to and during the trial of Emile Hebert are narrated, the words "Negro" and "colored" are used instead of Black and African American to reflect the vernacular of the period in which these events occurred. The word "Creole" here denotes Black residents of Louisiana who are of mixed African, colonial French, Spanish, and perhaps Native American ancestry. Originally used to mean people of mixed descent, "Creole" does not always indicate people of African heritage, but in this period and location, that was typically how the word was used.

7. Many sources incorrectly list him as "Achille Figaro," though his full legal name was Thomas Archille Figaro.
8. United Daughters of the Confederacy Alfred Mouton Chapter, Legal Documents 1870–1980, Box 1, File 6, Louisiana Room Collection, Edith Garland Dupré Library, University of Louisiana at Lafayette, Lafayette, LA.
9. In another ironic and historic twist of events, in 1908, Naomi Eleanor Figaro, the nineteen-year-old granddaughter of Jean Figaro, boarded a train to Lake Charles, Louisiana, and became the first teacher for Black Catholics in that community. She later helped to establish what would become the all-black Sacred Heart High School in Lake Charles.

CHAPTER ONE

That afternoon, Emile Hebert had no reason to think of rain. There wasn't a cloud in the sky. It was typically hot and humid for late June in south Louisiana, but the twenty-six-year-old Negro farmer was used to that. When he visited his father the week before, he had promised that he would return in a few days to help cut the first crop of okra. So, on the afternoon of June 20, 1922, Emile hitched his horse to the buggy and made preparations for the visit. His wife, Leona, packed food and milk for their three-month-old son, Lloyd. They would travel from Youngsville, a rural community in Lafayette Parish, to visit Emile's parents, who lived just north of Youngsville in an unincorporated part of Vermilion Parish.

Emile was the fourth oldest of the thirteen children of Victor and Victoire Hebert. At six feet, two inches, he was a handsome man whose mixed Creole and mulatto ancestry was evident in his light brown complexion and coarse, wavy hair. His thick eyebrows were particularly distinctive.

When the United States entered the Great War, Emile had volunteered to serve along with his brother John, fighting with the Allied forces in France. He had returned from the war a decorated soldier, determined to start a family and establish a good life close to his parents. In 1921, Emile had married his sweetheart, Leona, and they soon welcomed a son, Lloyd. Still, Emile's settled life was not always quiet. Like his father and older brothers, he was known for being outspoken and fearless of white men who threatened to harm him.

Just as Emile and his wife were preparing to return home after visiting Emile's parents, the rain started and poured heavily long past sunset. By the time the dark clouds cleared and the moon and stars appeared, it was nearly ten o'clock.

About the time that Emile set out, Lafayette Parish Sheriff Felix Latiolais was returning from nearby Abbeville, accompanied by Austin P. Landry, a prominent resident of Rayne, and Julius Delahoussaye, a local racehorse jockey. While driving down the mucky road, the sheriff's Model T got bogged down. After several unsuccessful attempts to push the stalled vehicle out of the ankle-deep mud, the men walked a half-mile to the nearby sugar refinery, where they found the Broussard brothers, Raymond and Jules, at work. The brothers provided hand tools and agreed to join the men to help clear the car. As the group made their way back, Julius left the road and cut across the cane field, taking a shorter route to check on the vehicle.

Shortly after eleven o'clock, Emile, with Leona sitting beside him and the baby asleep in her arms, met the four men walking in the middle of the narrow road.

"Please move over. I need to pass," said Hebert.

All but the sheriff moved to the side of the road.

"Move over?" Sheriff Latiolais said, laughing. "Boy, you're just what we need to get that 'T' over yonder out of the mud. We'll move when you get your ass down here and come help us push."

"Please, sir, I need to pass," Hebert replied.

"Where you going, boy? What's your hurry? Won't be much trouble for you to come with us and help push the car."

"I'm going home. Please get out of my way. It's late. I need to get my wife and baby to the house. I need to pass. I don't want trouble."

Enraged now, the sheriff shouted and prodded the spade in his hand in Emile's direction. "Look, you filthy, stinking nigger. If you don't get your ass down here, I'll reach up there and take you down. And I'll whip you so bad that no one will recognize you. Get your ass down here right now and come help us push."

Emile, angered by the sheriff's remarks and sensing the danger, released the reins, reached for his shotgun, and aimed it toward the men. "I need to get to the house. Move, you son of a bitch."

Backing away from the buggy, Sheriff Latiolais slung the spade, hitting Leona in the head. She and the baby tumbled to the muddy ground. The horse bucked and the buggy rolled. Leona screamed. In the frenzy, Emile stood up and fired his gun. Pellets splattered, hitting Austin Landry below the heart and across his abdomen. As the sheriff pulled his revolver and fired, Emile fired a second shot, hitting the sheriff in his side and striking Jules Broussard in the forehead and chest. Raymond Broussard ducked back into the field as Hebert started shooting and escaped without injury. Emile hurriedly gathered his wife and child back in the buggy and drove off.

Broussard ran quickly back to the refinery and called the deputy sheriffs in Lafayette, who contacted authorities in Youngsville. Delahoussaye, who had heard the gunshots, ran back to the road. Finding Austin Landry unconscious and Sheriff Latiolais and Jules Broussard bleeding badly, he attempted to tend to the injured men.

After arriving at the scene of the shooting, the deputies and Youngsville officials took the injured men to the office of a local doctor. On their way to Hebert's farm, they stopped to arrest John Hebert, Emile's brother. John was known to have a hot temper—one that the men feared could result in more violence. After arresting John, the men went to the home of Victor Hebert, Emile's father, to confirm Emile's whereabouts the evening before the shooting.

Standing six feet, five inches tall and of mulatto complexion, fifty-six-year-old Victor Hebert had an imposing stature. He had married his wife Victoire, commonly referred to as Cecile, in 1887. They had thirteen children, nine boys and four girls. The youngest was eight years old. Victor was known for meeting any threat to his family head-on. Once, when he was threatened by the KKK, he walked through Youngsville with a sign posted on his back that read, "Kick me if you can, but be prepared to leave your foot behind." On another occasion, upon hearing that the Klan planned to go to his farm to whip and perhaps lynch him and one of his sons, Victor positioned several of his boys in a ditch by the road in front of his house, armed with weapons, while his other children waited with loaded weapons in and around the house.

Finding Victor Hebert feeding his hogs, the marshal questioned him.

"Are you the father of Emile Hebert?" the marshal asked.

"*Oui.*"

"Did you see him yesterday evening? Did he visit you at your farm?"

"*Oui*, he come to help cut the okra. He and Leona left late 'cuz of the storm." Victor paused. "Where is Emile? What's wrong?"

The marshal said nothing more and the men drove off. Within minutes, the posse grew to four carloads of law enforcement officials, including police officers from Lafayette.

Meanwhile, Emile raced to the home of Charley Harrison to tell him about the incident. Also colored, Charley Harrison was Emile Hebert's age and had known him since childhood. Fearing that he would be hanged immediately if he was arrested with the shotgun in his possession, Emile had tossed the gun in a field before arriving at Harrison's residence. He told Harrison where the gun could be found before leaving to take his family home to safety.

The men arrived at Emile's farm shortly before dawn. Only the sound of roosters crowing could be heard in the calm, damp air. Emile had cleaned the buggy and put the muddy clothes in the horse trough to soak. He was coming out of the barn when the posse drove up.

The men stepped out of the cars and drew their weapons.

"Emile Hebert, stop right there," shouted the marshal with his rifle pointed at Emile. "Raise your hands. Let me see them, right now, damn it! Get down on your knees. Let me see your hands. Now!"

Emile obeyed the marshal's commands without speaking a word. Showing no fear or anger, he calmly surrendered.

"Where's your wife?" asked the marshal, as the deputies rushed toward Emile to handcuff him and put him inside the marshal's car.

"Leona and the baby inside, sleeping."

Several of the men rushed into the house, finding Leona in bed with her baby cuddled in her arms.

"Get up!" one of the deputies shouted, as men burst into the bedroom with pistols and rifles pointing inches away from Leona's face.

"Get up!"

"My baby! I have my baby!" said Leona, crying and screaming hysterically.

Still in her bedclothes, and with the baby in her arms, Leona was escorted out the front door, two men in front of her and two behind. She was placed in a separate vehicle.

While en route to the parish jail in Lafayette, the posse met Victor Hebert, who by then had gotten news of the shooting incident and was on his way to the jail, riding barefoot on horseback.

"Where is my boy? I heard about a shooting. What happened? Where's Emile?" Victor questioned.

"We have Emile and John Hebert in custody and are taking them to jail. Is this your son Emile?" asked the marshal, pointing at Emile in the back seat.

"*Oui*, that's my son Emile."

"When we saw you earlier, you said that Emile and his wife had gone to visit you yesterday evening. Is that correct?" asked the marshal.

"*Oui*, like I told you before, Emile and Leona come and stayed until the storm let up," Victor Hebert replied in a belligerent tone. "What happened, damn it?"

Giving no further details, the marshal and his caravan of town officials and law enforcement officers sped away.

Victor, furious now by the marshal's refusal to give details, and fearing for the safety of his children, gave one great kick to his horse and galloped toward Lafayette.

Leona was brought to the city jail, while Emile was confined at the parish jail. While in custody, Emile was told that Austin Landry had been pronounced dead. Emile showed no reaction to the news, staring silently and stoically into the marshal's face. Minutes later, he confessed to the crime.

———

On the afternoon of Emile's arrest, members of the Ku Klux Klan began gathering in Crowley, Louisiana, twenty-five miles away, to make plans to storm the Lafayette Parish jail, capture Emile, and hang him from the nearest tree. Shouts of "Nigger's gonna pay!" and "Hang that nigger!" rang out from the group.

Upon hearing of the gathering, District Court Judge William Campbell issued an order that Emile be immediately transported to the jail in Franklin, Louisiana, fifty miles south of Lafayette. He would be held there until shortly before his trial.

Since the 1830s, Franklin had been the home of many of the South's largest sugar plantations and had produced some of its wealthiest growers. With the development of steam boating, the town had later become an interior sugar port. Along Bayou Teche and Main Street stood some of the most beautiful and majestic plantation homes built during the antebellum era. Emile never saw them. It was an ironic twist of fate that, just a few blocks away, he was confined to the bitter darkness and sweltering summer heat of a narrow jail cell. The truth that he prayed would be uncovered was as hidden as the sweetness in miles and miles of cane, sprung up all around him, rising high above the heights of men, and stretching farther than eyes can see.

CHAPTER TWO

On August 24, 1922, two white men, Filmore Watt Daniel and Thomas F. Richards, disappeared from the face of the earth in Mer Rouge, a community of less than five hundred residents in Morehouse Parish. Rumor had it that the men, who had publicly spoken out against the Ku Klux Klan, had been kidnapped by the Klan. Several weeks passed, and the men were still missing. A staff assistant of Governor John Parker brought the incident to the governor's attention, but Parker's inquiries into the matter produced no answers. The governor was certain that in the course of his inquiries, his telephone had been tapped, and he had evidence that his telegraph and written correspondence to local law enforcement officials had been interfered with. He knew he needed to get federal officials involved.

John Parker had been born in 1863 in a village in south-central Louisiana and eventually became one of the wealthiest businessmen and planters in the whole South. After an unsuccessful run for governor in 1916 as a candidate of Theodore Roosevelt's Progressive Party, Parker ran again in 1920 as a member of the Democratic Party, this time winning on a platform advocating women's suffrage, abolition of child labor, and the levying of income and inheritance taxes. Parker had always hated the Klan, though few but himself knew the reason why. Many thought it was because his wife was Catholic. In truth, although Parker defended white supremacy, he abhorred the KKK's self-righteous philosophy and vigilante tactics. As a man of means, and a businessman at that, he believed each man had to earn his way in life.

Speaking in Lafayette at the dedication of the monument to General Alfred Mouton, Parker had praised the general as a man "who had the courage of his convictions and gladly gave his life battling for those principles for which we, of the South, firmly stood during the dark days of the Civil War." In a speech given later that night, Parker said that he opposed the KKK of the 1920s but would not oppose them if they were dedicated solely to the same ideal as the nineteenth-century Klan—namely, white supremacy.

On September 20th, nearly a month after the disappearance of the two white men in Mer Rouge, Governor Parker met with Paul Wooten, a correspondent for the *Times-Picayune*. The young news correspondent, who by then was already a seasoned reporter, had won accolades while heading the *Picayune*'s Washington, DC, bureau at the start of the Great War. Parker had requested the meeting to ask a special favor of Wooten, but had not disclosed the nature of it. Wanting to keep the meeting and conversation as secret as possible, the governor suggested that they stroll the grounds of the Governor's Mansion. They walked a meandering, graveled path at the rear of the mansion. Light fog still lingered as the sun barely peeped through the clouds.

Governor Parker walked slowly with his head down and his hands clasped behind him, as if he were weighing every thought and measuring the length of every step taken.

"Paul, I can't thank you enough for stopping by on such short notice. These groundskeepers really do a fantastic job here, don't they? It's a bit hazy out here but still a pleasant morning. If you don't mind, let's just stroll and chat."

"That suits me fine, Governor. It *is* pleasant out here," said Wooten, gazing down at the neatly kept lawn and bright-colored petunias and crossandras blooming in the gardens.

"Paul, let me say first of all that I think the *Picayune* is doing a mighty fine job of covering the KKK situation in north Louisiana," said the governor, stopping to look directly at Wooten. "Most newspapers around the state won't even refer to them by name."

"Thank you, Governor."

"This kidnapping in Mer Rouge is really troubling," said Parker, looking back toward the ground. He continued walking. "Would you believe that, with all the power and resources at my disposal, I can't get one straight answer from anybody up there? Two men are missing, presumably dead, and I can't get a single law enforcement agent or prosecutor in northeast Louisiana to tell me what on earth is going on. I get a lot of so-called rumored reports. But hell, this ain't New Orleans. We're talking about Mer Rouge. It's been a month since the kidnapping occurred. How long does it take to count a dozen eggs in a hen house? What the hell's going on up there?"

"Governor, our sources say the situation has really escalated," Wooten replied. "Klansmen are virtually governing Morehouse and Ouachita

Parishes. They've got the city halls, the courthouses, the jails, even the post office in Monroe."

"Well, tell me something I don't know, Paul. I know the foxes guarding the hen house. I've been in touch with everybody in northeast Louisiana who's carrying a seal or a badge in his wallet. They're all corrupt. Written replies to my inquiries are either anonymous or they've been opened before they arrive. The telephones are wired. Telegraphs don't work. Heck, the grand jury won't even convene. It's total anarchy up there. Who kidnapped those men, and why? I hear rumors about them being burned and dumped into a river. Why is it taking so long to find the bodies?"

Wooten suspected that the favor the governor wanted was related to the KKK activities in north Louisiana, but at this point a request hadn't been made. He listened and responded but couldn't help but wonder whether the governor merely wanted to find out what he knew about the missing men in Mer Rouge. "We have about as much information as you have, Governor. That's about all we know, that F. W. Daniel, Thomas Richards, and several other men were dragged from their cars by hooded Klansmen in broad daylight with hundreds of people watching. And, yeah, we've heard the same rumors, that Daniel and Richards were set on fire and their bodies were weighted down and dropped into a lake. But not a single witness has come forth."

"Well, rumors like that just don't drop from the sky. Who's the source? And why, Paul? What did these men do?"

"That's also anybody's guess, Governor," Wooten said. He turned to look at Parker, thinking that his assumption about the purpose of the visit might, in fact, be true. "We've heard that the men had spoken out against the Klan. We've also heard that a handful of hooded men decided to take law into their own hands to get rid of bootlegging and prostitution."

"Wearing hoods? Mother of Jesus! Paul, I honestly don't know how deeply the Klan has infiltrated. I'm told they're getting a lot of support from the outside, from Georgia and elsewhere. Judging by the lynchings up there, and the reports coming out of the district courts, we clearly are in a crisis situation. These outrages have got to stop. And you know, it's necessary that we deal with all this virulent behavior, because we've got good, decent people here. It's important that we not let the rest of the country believe that the whole doggone state is being controlled by the KKK, because it's not."

"I couldn't agree with you more, Governor. You're doing the right thing to speak out and take a stand against the Klan. But you're walking a thin line here. We need the public sentiment, but you also have to convey a positive message that the decent people of Louisiana and the state government are in control."

Sighing, the governor continued. "I'll never admit this publicly, Paul, but it's getting to the point where I don't know who to trust. As far as north Louisiana is concerned, everybody in authority seems to be wearing a hood, a mask, or a shady-looking smile. The Klan is spreading like a wildfire in the pines."

"Indeed, they are," Wooten responded.

"And they've begun to crop up in the southwest and south-central regions. Pretty soon every cousin on my Christmas list will be wearing a hood and burning crosses. One day, I'll get my hands on a list of names and flush out the whole stinking cesspool."

"Yeah, it's surprising that they've grown so quickly in the south, especially in the Acadiana parishes with so many Catholics. Speaking of which, are you familiar with the Hebert murder case in Lafayette Parish?"

Distracted by a large flock of birds passing overhead, Parker paused and looked up. "Is that the young Negro who was involved in a shootout with the sheriff?"

"Yes, sir."

"Well, I remember reading about it when it happened a couple of months ago. Has Judge Campbell set a trial date?" asked the governor, still looking at the birds.

"Not that I'm aware of, but it should come up soon after the court reopens in a few weeks. We'll be covering it. Tension is really building. According to our sources, there's a coalition brewing between the sugar growers and the Klan to incite violence. Vigilantes have already made one attempt to overtake the jail. Rumor is they'll try again."

Looking back at Wooten, the governor replied, "Why the heck are the growers meddling in that?"

"I'm not sure, Governor."

"I wonder if my friend Senator Broussard is aware."

"How do you mean, sir?"

"You know, Edwin's from New Iberia. That's in his backyard. He's the strongest supporter the sugar growers have in the US Senate. He's advocated a higher tariff on sugar since he first set foot on Capitol Hill. As a Roman Catholic, I'm sure he wouldn't be happy to hear that the growers have aligned with the KKK, even if it's clandestine. The Klan really went after Edwin in his bid for senate. There's no love there, I assure you. Edwin is also a close political ally with Percy Ogden, the prosecutor down there." After a slight pause, the governor continued, "Who's handling the defense, Paul? Do you know?"

"An attorney name John Kennedy."

"John L. Kennedy . . . a brilliant trial lawyer. Sounds like a real powder keg. I'm sure Percy Ogden will find a way to set it off. Keep me informed on that, will you?"

"Be happy to, sir."

Governor Parker stopped walking and gestured to Wooten to join him in taking a seat on a bench. Turning toward Wooten, the governor cleared his throat and his voice fell. "Paul, back to the Mer Rouge situation. You know, this . . . uh, this problem up there, this interference with communications is pretty serious. I've got to get the Feds involved. I've drafted a letter to the US attorney general, asking him to dispatch some federal agents to come down here and look into all this, including Klan violence in general. But I've got another problem. I need to be absolutely sure that the attorney general gets the letter and that no one reads it before it gets to his office. I can't chance sending it through the post office or the telegraph company. It's all run by Klansmen or their sympathizers. Paul, can I impose on you to get this done, to hand-carry this letter to the Justice Department?"

Realizing the governor's reason for the meeting and the favor he wanted, Wooten graciously obliged. "Well, most certainly, Governor. I'd be honored. How soon do you need it delivered?"

"As soon as possible. The situation is most urgent. I've already made contact with the congressmen of the 4th and 5th Districts in central and north Louisiana, although I'm not so sure whose side they're on. I'll also speak to Senator Broussard. It's my understanding that Senator Ransdell is on his way to Washington as we speak."

Thinking briefly, Wooten asked, "Where is the state legislature in all this, Governor?"

Governor Parker chuckled. "That's a darn good question. Where are they? Hiding behind some tree, I suppose, or engaging in their usual backroom 'klanversations' about my so-called obsession with eradicating red-blooded Americanism. Remember Senator Dreyfus's bill a year ago to outlaw wearing masks in public? Hell, he exempted Mardi Gras and still couldn't get the bill out of committee. Remember the jokes about outlawing Santa Claus, the Easter Bunny, and Halloween? That's how serious they take this. I tried to push a bill a few weeks ago to require fraternal organizations to register and list their members with the Secretary of State. They killed that too.

"Paul, one other thing. Knowing what you now know about the communication problem at the Monroe post office, if you happen to go knocking on the door of the chief post office inspector while you're in Washington, you'd be doing a great service to the state."

"I'd be happy to do that as well, Governor."

Before Parker stood up, he reached into his coat pocket and handed Wooten a sealed envelope. The governor then stood, and Wooten followed. "You're a fine gentleman, Paul," said Parker, as the two men shook hands. "I can't thank you enough."

"Well, I best be getting started. You have a good day, sir," said Wooten, as he started walking toward the front of the mansion.

"Oh, and Paul?" the governor called.

"Yes, Governor?" said Wooten, stopping to look back.

"Just out of precaution, please stress to anybody you talk to up there in either the Justice Department or with the chief postal inspector, that down here we don't hunt birds with a brass band marching behind us. Any federal contact with Louisiana law enforcement or judicial officials, state or local, must come through me initially—face to face."

"I understand, Governor. I most certainly will."

———

Five days later, Wooten handed over the governor's letter to J. Edgar Hoover, then assistant director of the Bureau of Investigation of the Justice Department. Later that day, Hoover sent a memorandum to the bureau's director, William J. Burns, notifying him of the details of the letter. In his note, Hoover wrote, "The governor has been unable to use either the mails, telegraph, or telephone because of interference by the Klan. . . . The Postmaster at Monroe is understood to be a member, as are a number of prominent officials and businessmen."

CHAPTER THREE

After months of waiting, the trial of Emile Hebert was set to begin at the Lafayette Parish Courthouse on Monday, October 23, 1922, with the selection of the jury. Shortly after Hebert's arrest, with the sheriff of Lafayette incapacitated, a small band of men intending to hang Hebert had made plans to overtake the parish jail. Upon learning of the plot, District Court Judge William Campbell ordered that the prisoner be moved to a jail in St. Mary Parish. As the trial date drew nearer, rumors began to circulate that another plot was stirring among a much larger group of avengers to storm the courthouse, seize Hebert, and hang him before the trial. Judge Campbell felt compelled to bring the situation to the attention of Governor Parker and request his assistance. They met over coffee in the gardens at the Governor's Mansion, seated at a small, wrought iron table.

Distinguished by his thick handlebar mustache, Campbell would turn sixty-six years old in three days. A Tulane Law graduate, he had built an esteemed career in public service, having previously served as sheriff of Lafayette Parish, mayor of Lafayette, and district attorney of the 18th Judicial District. He had also established a reputation for being a staunch defender of the constitution.

"You know, Judge, I spend so much time meeting here at the mansion that folks have started asking if the legislature has bolted the door and changed the locks to my office at the Capitol," the governor said, while reaching down from his chair to pluck weeds from the flowers nearby.

"Well, you certainly can't find better refuge than among God's natural wonders," said Judge Campbell, gazing at the pristine, lush landscaping of the grounds.

"Except when alligators and snake-bellied men crawl out of the swamp and try to bite you on the tail."

Judge Campbell laughed hard, but just as quickly returned to a stern expression behind his thick mustache and reserved demeanor, letting the governor know that he was there to discuss very serious business.

"Governor, I know you are aware of the situation we have in Lafayette with the Hebert trial. The trial starts in a week, and I've heard that a large number of protesters are threatening to take Hebert out of jail and hang him. They plotted to overtake the jail shortly after Hebert's arrest. Fortunately, I got word of it in time and ordered that he be moved to Franklin in the custody of Jailer Boudreaux and his deputies. I'm told that their number has now grown into the hundreds . . . perhaps as many as five hundred. Even with law enforcement officers of surrounding parishes, we're pitifully ill-equipped and undermanned to handle a mass raid. The situation is extremely volatile."

Governor Parker poured both men a cup of coffee from a silver pot that a servant had placed on the table shortly before the meeting. "Well, have the law enforcement officials been able to identify who the leaders are and whether any local officials are involved?"

"The only information that's come forward is that the KKK is instigating, but as you know they operate like a fraternal order. No one talks to the outside."

"You know, I tried to break that barrier with a bill requiring them to register their members every six months. My friends in the legislature thought it was a bad idea, of course. So, this trial is only a week away. Percy Ogden is going to have his hands full with this one. I'm told that John L. Kennedy is handling the defense."

"Well, we'll see. I'm sure they'll both be well prepared. You know, Governor, history does have a strange way of circling."

"How do you mean, Judge?"

"Well, it was General Fred Ogden, one of Percy's ancestors, who in 1874 led the White League militia that overtook the state house in New Orleans. The White League was about as vicious as the Klan is today. President Grant eventually sent troops and warships to restore Governor Kellogg back to power, but former White Leaguers played a large role in trying to regain white supremacy in the southern parishes."

"Oh yes, the Battle of Liberty Place. Heck, I was in Presbyterian boarding school when that happened. Yes, history does seem haunting at times."

"And now Percy himself is caught in the middle of a liberty battle, of sorts—as we all are, I suppose—to hold back a threatening revolt. Let's hope he's on the right side of history."

"I pray to God we all are." The governor paused and walked several feet to pull more weeds from the garden. His plucking weeds from the flowers reminded him of his father, a cotton broker who not only sold cotton but also traded slaves. "My daddy, bless his soul, never picked cotton a day of his life, but he sure knew how to sell it. Every time I pull tares from these flowers, I think about him buying and selling slaves for plantation owners needing to get their crop planted and picked."

Parker reached for a napkin and wiped his hands as he sat back down. "Judge," he said, reaching for his cup, "I was meeting with Paul Wooten of the *Picayune* recently, and he mentioned that the sugar growers had gotten involved in the situation in Lafayette, apparently backing the KKK. My Lord, we haven't seen that kind of racial violence in the sugar parishes in twenty years. It seems to me that the KKK is desperately trying to fuel the flames wherever they can and use this case to grow their numbers among Catholics . . . whom they absolutely hate, of course. It's the most absurd thing I've ever heard. At any rate, I've alerted Senator Broussard to what's going on."

"I'm surprised the Klan's grown so rapidly in south Louisiana," said Judge Campbell. "I hear they've got chapters in Lafayette, Opelousas, Iberia, Crowley—even as far west as Calcasieu Parish. If they can overtake law enforcement in Lafayette and lynch Hebert, it would certainly show their strength and add to their numbers."

Calm and reserved, Judge Campbell spoke in a monotone. He had yet to mention the real purpose of his visit, but knowing of Parker's staunch opposition to the Klan and his determination to end their dominance in the state, Campbell was patient to let the governor vent his frustration and anger about the Klan's growing power and influence. As the governor spoke, Campbell uncrossed his legs and poured himself another cup of coffee.

"And in every hog pen the KKK feeds, they find public officials to wallow in it," said Governor Parker, with his voice rising. "They can't be invisible unless they find enough law enforcement officers to get under the sheets with them. That's my concern, Judge. How many police and public officials in the southern parishes have been corrupted with the Klan's money or whatever else they are using to cover up their virulent behavior?"

"I'm sure there are some," said the judge, stirring his coffee. "A few days ago, I issued a public statement to the grand jury at the opening of the court, in which I directly addressed that issue, that public corruption and nonenforcement of any laws in this district will not be tolerated. All the newspapers in the area printed it, so the message got out."

Governor Parker rose from his chair and again looked down at the garden, thinking about Judge Campbell's statement while wondering why the groundskeepers had not tended to the flowers. While in thought, he was drawn into the bright glare of the mid-morning sun, which was now starting to beam down on both men. As Parker gazed silently at the sky, Campbell remained seated, looking aimlessly at his cup.

"Yes, I was sent a copy of your statement, Judge," Parker responded. Still looking up at the sun, a trace of resolve crossed the governor's face, yet in his heart he feared for the heart and soul of Louisiana. "Judge, I really believe we are at a critical juncture in our state's history. We are wrestling here with powers that threaten our basic goodness and the very fundamentals of orderly government. The very tenets of our state creed and our belief in the principles of union, justice, and confidence are at stake." The governor looked down toward Judge Campbell and placed a hand on his shoulder. "Unfortunately, there aren't enough judicial officials like you who have the courage to speak those kinds of words publicly. We clearly don't have any in north Louisiana."

Judge Campbell, whose thoughts were mainly on the upcoming trial and rumors of violence that would prevent a trial from taking place, stood to face Parker. "Thank you, Governor. But what's needed here now is something much stronger than words. I'd like you to deploy the National Guard to stand ground at the courthouse during the Hebert trial."

The governor winced. "National Guard? Judge, that's a pretty drastic measure. You think the mob situation is that threatening?"

"Yes, I do. And I think we need a forceful deterrent, not just a few pistol-carrying deputies."

"Calling the National Guard out for a criminal trial!" Parker exclaimed. "My God, that's unprecedented. But if it's as bad as you say, with a mob threatening to hang Hebert before the trial takes place, having the Guard there might be a good thing, particularly in light of all that's happening in north Louisiana and the movement of the KKK into the south. I think the presence of the troops would send a clear and resounding message to the Klan that they've gone far enough. Masked men and invisible empires have no place in our state."

"I agree, Governor. Whether Hebert is guilty or innocent must be determined by a trial in the court of law, not by a lynch mob of the KKK."

"God knows we don't need another Mer Rouge on our hands," said Parker. "It's been nearly two months now and they still haven't found the bodies of those men. I've asked the Bureau of Investigation to go up there. Between you and me, I'm planning a trip to Washington next month to personally meet with President Harding. We need federal help to bring some order amidst the chaos. We can deal more effectively with our local situation if we can cut off the support and encouragement the Klan is getting from the outside. But the last thing I want to do is send a message that the state is not in control."

"Well, I think having the troops at the Hebert trial will be a good step in that direction. We're grateful for your support."

"Thank you, Judge, for your decency and courage," said Parker, extending his hand to shake Campbell's. "I'll call Adjutant General Toombs immediately and issue the command. Feel free to get with him to work out the particulars."

CHAPTER FOUR

Two days before the start of the trial, US Senator Edwin Broussard held a private meeting of major sugarcane growers in the region to discuss rumors of their alignment with the KKK in the plot to overtake the jail and hang Hebert. A former educator, army veteran, and prosecutor, Broussard had been born in the village of Loreauville, located in rural Iberia Parish. Like Governor Parker, he was a former loyalist of Roosevelt's Progressive Party and had, in fact, run on Parker's ticket for lieutenant governor in his first campaign for governor. In 1920, Broussard was successful in filling the seat vacated by his brother, Robert F. Broussard, after he died. Accompanying the senator was District Attorney Percy Ogden.

Around 10:00 a.m., Senator Broussard walked inside the barn of one of the growers and was greeted by the owner. Stepping onto stacked bales of hay and overlooking a gathering of nearly three dozen men, Broussard opened the meeting.

"Gentlemen, thank you all for coming. For those who don't know me, I'm US Senator Edwin Broussard, and I am proud to represent this great state. I'm sure you know our distinguished district attorney of the 18th Judicial District, Mr. Percy Ogden," said Broussard, gesturing toward Ogden.

As prosecutor, forty-four-year-old Percy T. Ogden had never lost a murder case. He was a brilliant orator who had campaigned for several governors. A rising political star with ambitions of higher public office, Ogden was keenly aware that this trial would make or break his career and was determined to get a conviction.

After a smattering of applause, Senator Broussard continued. "Gentlemen, you will not find a more loyal friend than me in the Senate. I have fought for your interest every single day of the two years that I have served, and I will continue to fight. Just this summer, Senator Ransdell and I joined with Senator Kendrick of Wyoming as the only—I repeat, the *only*—Democratic senators to vote for the Fordney-McCumber Tariff Act.

As I'm sure you are aware, this new law gives raw sugar the highest tariff rate increase of any commodity produced in the United States. In signing the bill a month ago, President Harding called it the greatest tariff law ever passed by Congress." The men applauded loudly.

Broussard removed his hat and suit coat and loosened his necktie while continuing to speak. "Now, I've asked you to come here because I've received some very disturbing information. I'm told, from a most reliable source, that some of you are in cahoots with the KKK to protest against a colored farmer—Hebert, I believe is his name—in the murder trial in Lafayette Parish." Gesturing with his arms extended and his hands open, the pitch of Broussard's voice rose. "I am in utter disbelief that, as devout and upstanding as I know you are in your Christian beliefs, you would stoop to sit at the devil's table.

"Now gentlemen, I am a Roman Catholic, as I'm sure most of you are, and because I am Catholic, I am hated by the Ku Klux Klan. You are, too, for that matter. They opposed my candidacy two years ago, and I have no doubt they will oppose my reelection bid in a few years. So, it greatly disturbs me when I hear a report that some of you have gotten in bed with the enemy. And I don't mean that as a metaphor. A lesser-informed constituent might even mistakenly associate my relations with you as condoning the immoral, satanic acts of the Klan."

Broussard's voice got louder. "So, will someone under this roof please tell me what the heck is going on?"

Broussard stepped down from the hay and began a slow walk closer toward the men. In a final plea for reason, he pointed to Percy Ogden and lowered his voice. "Now, Percy Ogden, a political ally who happens to be my friend, is a darn fine prosecutor. As many of you know, my brother Robert, rest his soul—who fought even harder for your interests than I do and whom I am honored to succeed in the US Senate—would not have been elected were it not for Percy, who traveled all across this state to speak on Robert's behalf. If you want justice, keep the scales of the snake's belly off your sheets and stand, not with the KKK, but with our most capable prosecutor Mr. Ogden. Stand with him. I have the greatest confidence that he will get the job done . . . as he always does."

Several of the men grumbled at the thought of leaving justice to the fate of a court trial. They clearly wanted to take the matter into their own hands and not see Hebert go to trial.

"Senator, with due respect," said one of the growers, "we've heard that this nigger has confessed to the shooting. What if he gets off?"

"Well, I think Mr. Ogden is going to see to it that he doesn't," responded Broussard.

"The evidence is compelling," Ogden interjected. "We have witnesses to the shooting. We have a confession. And we have the murder weapon that Hebert confessed to owning."

"But we're told that this nigger has been organizing sugar workers to strike," shouted another grower after spitting a glob of snuff to the ground.

"Told by whom—the KKK?" shouted Senator Broussard above the murmurs of the crowd. "Do you have proof of that? Listen, the Klan will say and do whatever it takes to accomplish their objective, which is to hang Hebert before the trial and grow their membership. My advice to you is to wash your hands of the matter. Let Percy Ogden do his job."

"I think all the nigger cane farmers around here are in cahoots to turn the gangs against us. The less we can harvest and sell, the more money they make. Letting one of them hang might be a good lesson to the rest of them!" another planter shouted from the rear, stirring the loudest applause of the gathering. Some raised fists in the air and shouted obscenities.

"I disagree," said Broussard. "The best lesson to teach every farmer, colored and white, is that they cannot commit murder without paying the ultimate price. If Percy does his job, as I know he is more than capable of, Hebert will be hanged—legally. And you can bet that every Negro in this area will think twice about defying the law and inciting resistance. I implore you. Let the judicial process run its course."

After Broussard ended his remarks, the men huddled closer together, mumbling to each other. Broussard walked through the crowd to shake hands, but few were extended.

CHAPTER FIVE

J ury selection for the trial of Emile Hebert began on October 23rd at the usual morning opening of the court. It was expected that the selection process would last at least a day. The trial would commence shortly thereafter. As the court deliberated, a mob of at least five hundred white men gathered behind a general store in Crowley, fifteen miles from Rayne, the hometown of Austin P. Landry. Their plan was to go to Lafayette, storm the jail, seize Hebert, and hang him before the start of the trial.

Armed with rifles and led by local leaders of the Ku Klux Klan, the crowd consisted largely of small farmers and laborers who had traveled from nearby towns. Shouts of "Let's go hang a nigger!" and "Let's make that nigger pay!" rang out. Several sugarcane trucks had been brought to transport the armed men in what would be a bold, public display of vengeance, marching through downtown Lafayette without fear of anyone stopping them.

While the mob gathered, forty-eight National Guardsmen of Company E Infantry at New Iberia rode into Lafayette and established camp on the grounds of the Lafayette Parish courthouse, pitching tents and stationing themselves outside and inside the courtroom. They were later joined by twelve members of Machine Company M of Lafayette. Visitors entering the courthouse were searched for weapons. It was the first time in the history of the parish that the military was deployed in connection with a trial.

That same evening, Hebert's defense attorneys, John L. Kennedy and Sidney Roos, met with Hebert's wife and father to discuss their defense strategy. The attorneys painted a grim outlook for an acquittal.

A tall, bearded man, fifty-one-year-old John L. Kennedy was the lead attorney and an experienced trial lawyer who had built a highly successful practice. He was also very respected among the Negro residents of the parish for having secured acquittals for colored people who had been falsely accused of a crime. Kennedy was a devoted family man and the father of five children, the youngest of whom was eight years old. His second daughter had died in 1907 at the age of two.

Victor Hebert had been very engaged in the case since the morning of his sons' arrest. He had personally sought Kennedy to defend Emile, knowing of Kennedy's devotion to his family and his reputation for defending colored people in criminal cases. He had also heard that Kennedy spoke and understood Creole French.

Kennedy began. "Mr. Hebert, testimony will start tomorrow. We've been told that a mob of hundreds of men from this region are plotting to prevent this trial from happening. Rumor has it that they plan to storm the jail or the courtroom, take Emile, and hang him from the nearest tree. As you know, the National Guard has staked out in the courthouse square to stop them."

"*Quitte yé pa pend mo legason*," said Victor. "Don't let them hang my boy."

"As Emile's defense attorneys, we're certainly going to do our best to prevent that," Kennedy replied. "Look, I took this case because I know Emile is innocent. I know in my heart, as you do, that Emile fired his weapon in self-defense. I know that Emile did what he felt he had to do at that moment for the life of his family. And I know that, in the eyes of Almighty God, there is no guilt or condemnation for what Emile did. But our challenge is to defend Emile's innocence in the eyes of men . . . in a court of men."

Sighing, Kennedy continued. "Folks, I don't want to be discouraging, but I don't want to give false hope either. I believe we have a chance to win, but I must be honest with you. Emile has some big strikes against him. Our chance of a not guilty verdict here is slim."

"But Emile shot to live. They woulda killed him," protested Leona, visibly distraught over the bleak picture that Kennedy painted of the possible outcomes of the trial.

"That they might have, Leona. At the very least, they would have nearly beaten him to death. But here's what we're up against. Number one, Emile's colored. I needn't tell you that Negro men in this state have been lynched for crimes far less severe than murder. Hell, most have been lynched for no crimes at all. Second, Emile has openly confessed to the shooting. Last, and most unfortunate for Emile's fate, the men he shot are white. One white man is dead, and two others are wounded, including the highest-ranking law enforcement officer in the parish. To make matters worse, at least two of the victims are witnesses to the shooting. For certain, the prosecutor will put the sheriff and Raymond Broussard on the witness stand. Jules Broussard may not be healthy enough to testify. The prosecution need only persuade the jury that Emile shot with the intent to kill those men. For a district attorney as experienced and skilled as Percy Ogden, and with such compelling evidence, that's not going to be hard to do."

Sidney Roos chimed in. "And Percy Ogden has to win this case. He can't afford to lose. Remember that Austin Landry, the deceased victim, is from Rayne in nearby Acadia Parish. That's Ogden's home parish. Many people suspect that Ogden has statewide political ambitions. For years, he's been stomping around the state making speeches for politicians, including several former governors. Losing this case could be extremely damaging to his political future. So, he's motivated by a lot more than seeing justice rendered."

"But the picture is not all doom and gloom," said Kennedy. "Emile does have a lot working on his behalf. For one, he's a decorated war veteran. He has no prior criminal record. He's a family man and a hard-working farmer. And most importantly, we have an honest judge, Judge Campbell, who just three weeks ago opened the court with a message to the grand jury that spoke strongly against corruption in law enforcement."

Kennedy reached for a newspaper clipping on the edge of his desk. "Let me read you some of the words the judge spoke. He said, 'There is no greater evil today than the nonenforcement by public officials of laws which they have sworn to uphold. Obedience to the rule of law is what sets this nation apart. The rule of law applies to all governments, all races, and all stages of the history of this nation, and when the laws are ignored, there is no government at all.' The judge went on to say, 'The government will endure on the rock of law enforcement or it will perish in the quicksand of lawlessness.' The judge is saying that no law enforcement official can choose to enforce some laws and ignore other laws. I also believe that he spoke those words with full knowledge that a number of judges, sheriffs, and prosecutors in the northern part of the state are closing their eyes, turning their backs, and, in many cases, outright participating in the vicious, terrorist acts of the KKK. Judge Campbell is saying that political corruption of that nature won't be tolerated in his jurisdiction."

"And so, our best defense," Roos joined in, "is to show that Emile is a good man, a war veteran with a young family, and that he acted purely in self-defense. Our second-best defense is to show that the sheriff is a liar and that it was him, and not Emile, who acted violently. He struck the first blow, hitting Leona with the spade and endangering the baby's life as well."

"That he did," said Kennedy. "I might even go so far as to connect Latiolais to the Ku Klux Klan, but I've got to be very careful with that. We don't know that to be a fact. We have no evidence beyond his campaign talk. And even if we did, we're still dealing with a very powerful and popular elected official. There's not a man or woman in this region who'd testify to the sheriff's involvement with the Klan. Before he was elected sheriff, Latiolais was Lafayette's first city marshal. To most people of this parish, he has served with honor and distinction. To put it plainly, we've got to pit good against evil—Emile against the sheriff and the KKK. We've got to make the case that a guilty verdict is equivalent to a lynching, not by the jury, but by Latiolais and the state.

"And speaking of the state, the National Guard is here because Governor John Parker gave the order at the request of Judge Campbell. The governor has also spoken out very strongly against the Klan's control of north Louisiana. Word is that he's asked President Harding to send federal investigators to north Louisiana to look into the disappearance of two white men who are suspected to have been kidnapped and killed by the KKK. If we lose, we'll appeal. Then the case will go to the court of appeals and, if necessary, to the state supreme court. If all fails, execution will rest in the hands of the governor."

"And we mustn't underestimate the power of decency," said Roos. "We're still selecting a jury, but we're expecting to have respected businessmen like P. J. and Fred Voorhies, men who don't take kindly to meanness and unkindness of any color. For certain, nearly all of the jurymen will be Catholic. The Klan hates Catholics as much as they hate Jews and Negroes. The jury foreman will likely be L. P. DeBlanc, who helped to organize a Lafayette branch of the National Council of Catholic Men with the help of our first bishop—Bishop Jeanmard. All of that works in Emile's favor."

"The Voorhies are good men," agreed Victor. "They know my family, me and my sons. *Yé connain nouzaut travaille dur. Nou pa fè traka.* They know we work hard. We don't make trouble." Victor then paused. "We know the hangmen. All the colored know them. You must stop them. *Quitte yé pa pend mo legason.* Don't let them hang my boy."

Victor glanced at Leona, who, with tears in her eyes, pleaded, "Please don't let them hang Emile."

"Again, we're certainly going to do our best," said Kennedy. "But I want you both to understand that even with a good judge and a half-decent jury, a not guilty verdict is a long shot. Though the burden is on the state to show that Emile acted with the intent to kill, we've still got to persuade nine of the twelve white jurors that two, maybe three, white victims—including a very popular elected official of this parish—are lying and that Emile is telling the truth.

"You should also be aware that there is another course of action the jury may take. They may vote to convict Emile on a charge of second-degree rather than first-degree murder. That would probably mean life in prison as opposed to execution. That will remain an option if and when we get into the appeals process . . . all the way up to the governor. And then there is always the possibility of a hung jury. That's when the jurymen simply can't reach a decision of guilt or innocence, and the judge declares a mistrial. The state would then have to decide whether it will try the case again."

Victor, confused, turned to look at Leona. "But why would they have another trial if Emile wasn't guilty?" asked Leona, rocking her baby back and forth.

"That will be up to state," said Kennedy. "They have that right under the law, but chances are they will not retry Emile unless they can bring enough new evidence to convince nine of the twelve jurymen that he is guilty without a shadow of doubt."

"I'd almost rule out the possibility of a mistrial," Roos interjected. "Even that would be seen as a defeat for Percy Ogden, though not as bad as a not guilty verdict. He's aiming for guilty on first-degree murder, hoping that, at worst, he'll get second-degree." Roos paused. "Now, about our testimony, we plan to call both of you to testify—you, Leona, as a witness to the incident, and you, Mr. Hebert, as a spokesman to Emile's character. I'll probably do the questioning. My guess is that Ogden won't cross-examine. He'll want the jury to see and hear as little of you as possible and get you off the stand quickly. And he'll want the jury to see his silence as a gesture of respect, so he'll put on his sheep's clothing. Besides, it's Emile that he wants up there, not you. My advice to you is to just be yourselves. Be natural. Speak what's in your heart. Speak the truth as you know it."

Kennedy moved to sit on the edge of his desk, facing Leona and Victor. "There is one other issue that you should be aware of. Though not related to the case directly, it could well be a deciding factor in the outcome. Mr. Hebert, have you ever heard of the sugar bowl parishes?"

"*Non.*"

"Well, in north Louisiana, farmers grow mostly cotton. Toward the southwest, you find mostly rice. But in south-central Louisiana, as you well know, farmers grow sugarcane, which is why the twelve parishes of south-central Louisiana, including Vermilion and Lafayette Parishes, are known as the sugar bowl parishes. The fact that Emile is a young Creole sugar farmer is another reason why the mob and many other men in this region want to see him hanged."

"*Je ne comprends pas,*" responded Victor. "I don't understand."

"I know. It's a little complicated. Let me try to explain. For many years, white sugar planters in south Louisiana have intimidated and controlled colored workers, sometimes with outright lynchings, the same way the cotton growers control coloreds in the north. Except that in the south, the tendency is to control and punish colored sugar workers legally—to convict and execute them through the courts—oftentimes for crimes far less serious than murder. When I say that white sugar growers try to control colored workers, what I mean is that it's important to the growers that colored gang workers work for the low wages that growers want to pay them. So, the big farmers use both lynch mobs and legal means to make Negro workers afraid to speak out or to organize and strike for higher pay. The problem is not as bad as it used to be, but it still accounts for some lynchings today in both the north and the south."

"But Emile don't work the gang," said Leona. "He's a farmer and he don't just grow sugar."

"I'm aware," Kennedy responded. "And you would think that Emile's small farm is no threat to the big growers. But that's precisely what makes Emile a threat . . . the fact that he is a small farmer, and a Negro, who the growers don't control. So, now you have a colored farmer who has killed a white man and shot the sheriff. And you have the KKK carrying the rope. They're determined to hang Emile, legally or illegally—through the courtroom or with a rope tied to a tree outside the parish courthouse. The way the big growers see it, Emile's execution would be a strong warning and a lesson taught to other Negro farmers in the region.

"The growers, even those outside of Lafayette and Vermilion Parishes, have a lot of influence. Ogden has already managed to get a big landowner, Alex Verot, on the jury. It's very likely that Eraste C. Landry, another big farmer, will be selected. Not that these men aren't honorable, but they could be influenced. I will say that Eraste Landry is a charter member of the local council of the Knights of Columbus, so his being a devout Catholic might actually work in Emile's favor. Acadia Parish, the home parish of Austin Landry, is rice country, but I'd bet my last dollar that the sugar growers have their hand in the mob that's gathering there, along with the KKK, of course. A lot of people want Emile dead, people who have the money and means to make it happen."

"*Kisa nousot va fè?*" asked Victor. "So what do we do?"

"*Eh bien, Monsieur, on va se battre*. Well, sir, we fight," said Kennedy.

CHAPTER SIX

As Judge Campbell had hoped in making the request to the governor, the National Guard's presence proved to be an effective deterrent. The mob made no attempt to overtake the courthouse or the jail, and the jury selection proceeded as scheduled.

Trial testimony was set to begin on the afternoon of October 24th. Anticipating a long day, Kennedy and Roos had packed lunches. When Judge Campbell adjourned the court for a short break before the start of opening statements, the two men went outdoors and sat on a wooden bench beneath a canopy of magnolias. They talked about the case, particularly Ogden's strategy.

In the course of the conversation, Kennedy's attention was drawn to a large flock of blackbirds nesting inside a mulberry tree near the courthouse entrance. The weather had cleared, and large crowds were still entering the building. The presence of people stirred the blackbirds up badly, causing everyone walking toward the entrance to dodge the waves of fluttering thrush.

"Seems like those damn birds are the vigilantes we feared would stop this trial," Kennedy said, looking up at the trees. "Look at them, loud as hell and swarming everywhere."

"Maybe it's the KKK," joked Roos. "They do come in disguises." He paused briefly. "Are you ready?"

"About as ready as can be. As usual, I've made some notes, but I've got to wait and see the direction Ogden takes. Knowing him, he'll get dramatic at some point. I'll need a little of that myself."

As the men ate, Kennedy grew quieter and took fewer bites. Periodically looking into the mulberry tree, he settled into deep thought.

"Well, we best hurry," said Roos. "If Ogden gets his way, this might be the last meal of the day that we'll enjoy."

"I've had enough," Kennedy said. "Ready when you are."

The men rose to go inside the courthouse, swatting at blackbirds diving toward them as they made their way into the building.

Flanked by armed deputies, Emile Hebert entered the courtroom bound in handcuffs and shackles and was seated at a table with his two attorneys. Seated at another table opposite of the center aisle was District Attorney Ogden. Holding her baby, Leona sat with her father-in-law on the first bench behind the defense table. The jury sat to the right of the witness stand. The rest of the courtroom was standing room only. Most of the people there were white, but a small group of colored people, largely family members and friends of Emile, sat together in a section at the back of the room. National Guardsmen stood at the front, sides, and rear. Rain pounded on the roof, while the low boom of thunder could be heard in the distance. Judge William Campbell entered.

"All rise," said the bailiff. "The State of Louisiana versus Emile Hebert. The Honorable Judge William Campbell presiding."

"Thank you. Be seated please. Before we begin this trial, I think it would be appropriate to make a statement about the unusual circumstances surrounding these proceedings. As I said to the grand jury at the opening of this court several weeks ago, we are guided and governed by the eternal laws of justice to which we are subject. Government is a trust, and as officers of the government we are trustees, not of our own will but of the sovereign will of the people. In this high calling, it is as much our duty to protect justice as it is to live by it. Never before in the history of this court have we had to guard our doors. Never before has it been necessary for the National Guard, or any militia or law enforcement for that matter, to stand watch on our grounds. I want to be clear. I have asked the National Guard to be here in the interest of justice—to guard the sacred right of due process guaranteed by the constitutions of our great state and country. I fully expect those citizens present and those standing on the grounds of this courthouse to respect and uphold the law. Any conduct to the contrary will be dealt with sternly and swiftly. With that said, Mr. Ogden, you may present your opening statement."

Ogden walked toward the jurymen and faced them. "Gentlemen of the jury, we have spent a day and a half selecting you twelve fair-minded men, whom we pray will bring justice to the tragedy and horror that struck our region on the night of June 20th. Emile Hebert has confessed to killing Austin P. Landry, a prominent resident of Acadia Parish. He has also admitted to firing the shot that seriously injured Jules Broussard of Youngsville, that same shot that hit the honorable sheriff of Lafayette

Parish, Sheriff Felix Latiolais, and may well have rendered him incapable of fulfilling his elected duty.

"As witnesses will swear, Emile Hebert, a veteran marksman trained in the use of firearms, pointed a shotgun at Austin P. Landry at short range, pulled the trigger without warning, and hit the victim below the heart. As the sheriff shot, Hebert fired again with the intent to kill the entire party in distress, including Jules Broussard and his younger brother Raymond, who escaped unharmed.

"Hebert's defense will attempt to discredit the witnesses. They will say that Emile was threatened and provoked. But, gentlemen, I say to you that fear and provocation can be no excuse. Under no circumstances can they justify the taking of innocent life. I will prove beyond a shadow of doubt that Emile Hebert shot maliciously with cold, deliberate intent to kill . . . and that he did. Jurymen, this is more than a question of Hebert's guilt or innocence. It is a test of your moral courage to do what is right and to conclude that Emile Hebert should be hooded, noosed, and dropped from the gallows at a crystal blue high noon for the murder and mass assault he has committed and confessed to."

As Ogden took his seat, John L. Kennedy stood and strode toward the jury.

"Mr. Kennedy, your statement," Judge Campbell prompted.

"Thank you, Your Honor. Honorable men of the jury, you will hear testimony of the defendant that will clearly conflict with testimony of the state's witnesses. You will see and hear the defendant's remorse for the life lost and bodies injured in the shooting that took place, and you will hear him say with his own words that he felt no malice toward the men he encountered that terrifying night near Sugar Mill Road.

"Yes, gentlemen, Emile Hebert has admitted to firing the fatal shot that ended the life of Austin P. Landry. But you will hear Emile say that he first aimed his gun to give a warning when he felt that his life and those of his family were in danger. He shot, as any man would, to defend himself and his wife and child, barely three months old. Even now, the defendant fears for his life. It is common knowledge that shortly after Emile and his wife Leona were arrested, vigilantes plotted to overtake the jail. In his wisdom, our honorable judge moved Emile fifty miles to the Franklin jail. Judge Campbell also acted prudently in asking our governor to deploy sixty National Guardsmen of Company E, who were later joined by twelve members of Machine Company M, to cover the grounds of the courthouse during this trial . . . it being rumored that a mob of men from Acadia Parish had already started to gather and would try again to take the prisoner. Since yesterday morning, in a heavy downpour, the guardsmen have stood watch on the courthouse square. Even now, they stand armed at our doors.

"And so, gentlemen, your task here is to discern between truth and untruth, and to be a judge, not just of the defendant's action, but of his character, his heart, and his intent. I have no doubt that truth will prevail, and with it, your good conscience in the face of the God you have sworn to."

During both opening statements, the jury listened attentively, but none of the men showed any display of emotion. Knowing that there was much more to be said and presented in what would probably be a two-day trial, they were anxious to hear testimony of the witnesses.

"Mr. Ogden, you may call your witnesses," Judge Campbell said.

"Your Honor, we call the Honorable Sheriff Felix Latiolais of Lafayette Parish to the stand."

A short, burly man, forty-four-year-old Latiolais had been sheriff of Lafayette Parish for eight years, having previously served as the city's first marshal. He had married into a prominent family; his wife, Louise, was the daughter of Agnon Edgar Martin, who served as the first school superintendent of Lafayette Parish. Latiolais was well-liked and known for being hard on crime, but he was also known to use his office to intimidate and punish those who opposed him politically. Many colored residents feared him.

Latiolais rose and walked up to the witness stand, where the bailiff was waiting. "Place your left hand on the Bible and raise your right hand," said the bailiff. "Do you swear to tell the truth, the whole truth, and nothing but the truth, so help you God?"

"I do," said the sheriff. Lowering his hand, he took the empty seat on the stand.

Ogden began his questioning. "Sheriff Latiolais, would you describe for us what you saw, heard, and did in connection with the shootings that occurred near the Youngsville sugar refinery on the night of June 20th?"

"My good friends, I am grateful to be alive to speak this truth. It was a horrifying night. I had gone to Abbeville with Austin Landry and Julius

Delahoussaye, the race jockey at the fairgrounds. The rain was heavy all evening. We were about a half-mile from the sugar refinery in Youngsville when my Model T stalled in the mud. The three of us walked to the refinery and secured the help of the Broussard brothers, Jules and Raymond. We also found a few tools to help with the mud. On the way back to the car, the four of us met Emile and his wife in the buggy. They were traveling on a path that crossed Sugar Mill Road about a quarter mile from where the car had stopped. Delahoussaye had already cut across the cane field to check on the car, so he wasn't with us.

"Emile demanded that we move over and give him the right-of-way, so we moved to one side to let him pass. We then asked Emile to stop and help with the car. He refused. He yelled and cursed, then he stood up, raised his barrel, and pumped a shot into young Austin Landry. I slung a spade at the buggy, then pulled my revolver. The spade struck Hebert's wife, who fell to the ground with the baby. I barely let go a shot before Hebert fired again, hitting Jules Broussard and me."

"Sheriff Latiolais, how would you describe Emile's state of mind at the time of the shooting?"

"As I said, he yelled and cursed and demanded that he have his way. I tell you, his rage was like a bonfire. But that's not surprising for him. Many know about Emile's quick temper. On many occasion, I've been summoned to fights at the colored gambling shack in Broussard, oftentimes involving Emile and his brothers, not to mention times they disrespected good upstanding white people of this parish."

Kennedy stood up and shouted, "Objection, Your Honor."

"Sustained. The jury shall disregard the last statements made by the sheriff. Sheriff, if you would, please restrict your remarks to the questions asked. You may resume, Mr. Ogden."

"Sheriff, you said Emile raised his barrel and shot. Do you know what type of weapon he used?"

"Yes, he shot with a 12-gauge pump shotgun. You don't see many in these parts. Once you cock the trigger, every pump is a buckshot blast."

"And Sheriff," continued Ogden, moving as close to the sheriff as the partition in front of the witness stand would allow, "would you say that, generally, someone armed with such a weapon is fully aware of the deadly power of its force?"

"I would think so, yes."

"You said that Emile shot Austin Landry first and shot again after you threw the spade and reached for your revolver, and that he hit you and Jules Broussard with the second shot?"

"That's correct."

"What distance would you say Emile was from the distressed party when he fired these shots?"

"Oh, I would say no more than ten or fifteen feet."

"Close enough, would you say, that you could clearly see Emile and hear any words he spoke, and that if he issued a warning, either verbally or by pointing his gun, you would have seen or heard it?"

Latiolais nodded. "Yes, even in the dark I could see the twitch in Emile's eyes. We were that close. But we got no warning from him." The sheriff paused, his voice rising. "Only his fit of rage. I swear, he was like a madman."

Turning toward the jury now, Ogden asked, "So, you say that Emile did or said nothing to warn you and the other men that he would shoot?"

"No, he didn't, but he did swear and curse obscenities," Latiolais responded, more calmly.

"And do you recall any of these obscenities that Emile shouted?"

"He spoke a lot of vulgar. I don't remember all, but I distinctly recall him saying, 'If you white S.O.B.s don't get out of my way, I'll run over you.'"

"And this was said after you and the men had given Emile the right-of-way and asked him to get down and help with the car?"

"That's correct."

"Sheriff, you said that you and the men were ten to fifteen feet from the buggy when Emile fired. Given your experience as a law enforcement officer, would you say that a man who would aim and shoot a 12-gauge pump shotgun at someone at that close range would do so with intent to kill?"

"Cleary, if he wanted to warn, he could have shot away, in the air. But he pointed the barrel squarely at Austin and pumped the barrel. He wanted to kill. Then, he pumped and shot Jules and me."

"No more questions, Your Honor," said Ogden, returning to his seat.

Before Ogden sat down, Kennedy rose to cross-examine, walking slowly to the center of the courtroom.

"Sheriff, you said that when Emile demanded that you and the other men on the road give him the right-of-way, you cooperated and moved to the side of the road. You further said that Emile shouted obscenities when you asked him to get down from the buggy and help push the car out of the mud, did you not?"

"In so many words, yes."

"Sheriff, you seem to recall Emile's words quite well. Do you recall the exact words that you or any of the other men spoke to Emile when you asked him to get down from the buggy? And what was the tone and tenor of those words? Did you curse? Did you shout? Did you ask politely, or did you ask in a threatening way?"

"Objection, Your Honor," Ogden interjected.

"Overruled. Please answer the question, Sheriff."

"I don't recall every word. I asked politely at first. When Emile refused and started shouting obscenities, I told him to get his God damn nigger ass off the buggy or we'll take him off. That's when he raised the barrel and shot."

"And what exactly did you mean by 'take him off'?"

"I meant that I would reach up there and take him down. We needed a hand. It wasn't much to ask . . . not enough to kill a boy over, but enough to teach him a good lesson about being disrespectful."

"Sheriff, you said that after Emile shot the first shot, you threw the spade then drew your revolver. I believe those were your words. Are you absolutely, positively certain that you threw the spade after and not before Emile fired the first shot?"

"I am."

"And when did you see Leona and the baby fall off the buggy, before or after Emile fired the second shot?"

"I was caught up in defending myself and the rest of us. I didn't say I saw her fall from the buggy. I threw the spade and reached for my revolver. I caught a glimpse of the spade hitting the wife, but I didn't see her fall. As I fired my revolver, Emile shot again and hit me in the left side, barely missing my heart," said the sheriff, putting his right hand over his heart.

Kennedy moved close to the witness stand and placed both hands on the partition as he looked at the sheriff. "And did you see the horse buck and the wheel of the buggy roll over Leona and the baby when the spade was thrown?"

"I was caught up in a battle. I wasn't watching some damn mule or the wheel of some damn buggy." Several of the white residents in the courtroom laughed.

"One last question, Sheriff. As you know, the Ku Klux Klan have brought fear and terror to many communities and colored families in our region and state. The KKK tried to overtake our parish jail after Emile's arrest, no doubt to lynch him. It's been rumored that they will try again." Turning his back to the sheriff and glancing at the jury, Kennedy got to the question. "Sheriff, is it not true that in your bid to be reelected sheriff of Lafayette Parish two years ago, you publicly defended the terrorizing acts of the KKK?"

Rising to his feet, the sheriff pointed at Kennedy and shouted, "That's a damn lie, you white nigger," again drawing laughter from some white citizens in the courtroom.

Ogden stood up and yelled. "Objection . . . objection, Your Honor! That is unfounded . . . totally unconscionable!"

"Order! Order! Order in the court," said Judge Campbell, slamming his gavel four times. "Objection sustained. Mr. Kennedy, I needn't warn you of the consequences of one more stunt like that. And Sheriff, I must also caution you to bridle your tongue. You may continue, Mr. Kennedy."

"No more questions, Your Honor."

"Mr. Ogden, do you wish to redirect?"

"Absolutely, Your Honor," said Ogden, rising to step toward the sheriff. "Sheriff Latiolais, you say that you didn't see the horse buck and the wagon roll; but it would seem plausible, would it not, that a horse would buck from a shotgun blast coming from the rear quicker than he would buck from a small farm tool being hurled toward the buggy, would it not?"

"Yes, it would seem. It was probably Emile's own blast that stirred the horse and caused it to buck and move the buggy."

"Your Honor, I strongly object," shouted Kennedy. "That's all conjecture."

Ogden quickly jumped in. "Your Honor, that is no more conjecture than the preposterous and cockamamie story that the defendant will tell later . . . that he fired on these men after the sheriff threw the spade, after his wife fell to the ground, after the horse bucked, and after the wagon rolled. My witness is saying that it is just as plausible that it was the defendant's own action, not that of these men, that caused the buggy to roll over his wife."

"Objection overruled. You may continue, Mr. Ogden."

"No further questions, Your Honor."

"Mr. Kennedy?"

"No further questions."

Still standing, Ogden called his second witness. "Your Honor, the prosecution calls Raymond Broussard to the stand."

Raymond Broussard was sworn in by the bailiff and took his seat.

Slowly approaching the stand, Ogden began his line of questioning. "Raymond, you were a member of the party that met Emile near Sugar Mill Road the night of June 20th, were you not?"

"Yes, sir."

"Did you know Emile Hebert or his wife—had you ever seen or spoken to either of them before?"

"I'd seen him around, but I don't know him."

"And would you tell the court how you came to be involved in the tragedy?"

Twitching and rubbing the top of his head as he held a straw hat in his hand, Broussard looked visibly uncomfortable speaking in public. He spoke fast. "My brother Jules and me, we work the sugar refinery at night. The men came—Sheriff Latiolais, Mr. Landry, and the race jockey—and they said the car stalled in the road, and they needed hands to push. Jules and me went with them to help."

"And so, you and your brother Jules left with the other men to help push the car out of the mud?"

"Yes, sir."

"Raymond, would you tell the court what happened as you and the other men were walking down the road?"

"It happened the way the sheriff said . . . every word. We met Emile and his wife in a buggy. He told us to move over and let him pass, so we moved. Then the sheriff asked Emile to get down and come help with the car, and he started yellin' and cussin'. Then, he stood up in the buggy and pumped his gun. The boom of his blasts rattled my ears. The sheriff showed courage in throwing the spade and pulling his revolver, but it was no match for the 12-gauge pump raining down from the buggy. I was lucky to escape without injury."

"But your brother Jules was not so lucky, was he?"

Broussard lowered his head. "No, sir. He got hit in the forehead and the chest. He's alive, but still hurtin'."

"And when you said that he started yelling and cursing, you were speaking about Hebert, were you not?"

"Yes, sir."

"Raymond, did you see or hear Emile give any kind of warning to the men standing on the road before he stood up in the wagon and fired the first shot?"

"No, sir. Like the sheriff said, all Emile did was cuss."

Ogden glanced over to Kennedy and Roos, "Your witness."

With that, Sidney Roos rose and walked toward the witness stand.

"Mr. Broussard, where exactly were you standing in proximity to the buggy when Mr. Hebert started 'yellin' and cussin',' as you say?"

"When we started out, being the younger, I was walking in the back with the horse jockey. After a while, he left the road and went off to cross the cane field to go toward the car. So, I was standing behind the sheriff, Mr. Landry, and Jules when we met Hebert."

"How far behind?"

"I don't know, not far, a few feet I guess."

"And so, Mr. Delahoussaye, the race jockey, had walked across the sugarcane field and was not near the buggy at the time of the shooting?"

"No, sir."

"Mr. Broussard, at what point did you flee the scene after the shooting began, and how was it that you were not shot? How did you escape?"

"It all happened like a bolt of lightning, but I saw Emile stand up and raise his barrel at Mr. Landry's heart and fire the first shot, then I saw him pump a second blast. Pellets hit like hail on flesh and bone. The air was nothing but smoke and powder and men groaning. I threw myself into the ditch, then crawled through the cane field, fearing another round of pellets."

"So, after seeing a so-called madman stand up in a buggy with a shotgun and pump buckshots that scattered like hail, you stood still long enough to see the sheriff throw a spade and draw his revolver . . . and you stood still long enough to see this madman fire a second shot."

"Yes, sir."

"Well, I certainly admire your courage, Mr. Broussard. I would think that the average man who was unarmed as you were would have hit the ground or somehow tried to run for cover after the first shot."

"Objection, Your Honor," said Ogden, rising from his chair.

"Sustained."

Roos continued. "Mr. Broussard, you said you saw the sheriff sling a spade at the buggy. Did you see the spade hit Emile's wife and his three-month-old son, Lloyd, and did you see them fall off the buggy after Sheriff Latiolais hurled the spade?"

"Like I said, it's like asking me if lightning struck before or after I blinked. And it's the same with the question you asked Sheriff Felix about the horse bucking. I was watching a madman unload a 12-gauge pump, not some field tool or a horse."

"So, because lightning flashes so quickly, you cannot say with absolute certainty that the spade was thrown after the first shot?" Roos questioned, moving close to Broussard.

"I can only speak about what I saw."

"No more questions, Your Honor."

"Mr. Ogden, redirect?"

As Roos took his seat, Ogden stood but stayed close to the defense table, knowing that his redirect questioning would be brief. "Absolutely, Your Honor. Raymond, did you or did you not see Emile fire the first shot?"

"I did."

"And did you or did you not see the sheriff throw the spade and pull his revolver?"

"I did."

"And which occurred first, Emile's shot or the hurling of the spade?"

"Emile's shot."

"No further questions," said Ogden.

"Mr. Roos?"

"We have no further questions of the witness, Your Honor."

"You may step down, Mr. Broussard."

"Your Honor, the prosecution calls City Marshal Stutes of Youngsville as our next witness," said Ogden.

Marshal Stutes walked up to the witness stand and was sworn in.

Ogden started questioning his last witness, self-assured that the testimony of a second law enforcement official, and the one that had in fact arrested Hebert and taken his confession, would deal an unrecoverably damaging blow to the defense. "Marshal Stutes, you arrested Emile Hebert several hours after the killing, did you not?"

"Yes, I did, said Stutes with an aura of seriousness and confidence.

"Do you mind giving the court a full account of the arrest?"

Stutes spoke slowly, weighing his response carefully. "Upon hearing about the incident and going to the scene of the crime, I joined Mayor Parent of Youngsville and the two deputy sheriffs to go arrest John Hebert, one of Emile's brothers, as a precaution against more violence. Everyone knows his hot temper. We then went to see Victor Hebert, Emile's father, who lived in Vermilion Parish a mile or so north of Youngsville, and inquired as to Emile's whereabouts that evening before the shooting took place. When reinforcements arrived, we set out to arrest Hebert. We arrived at his residence around five o'clock that morning, at which point we found Emile coming from the barn. The wife was asleep in the house. Hebert surrendered without resistance."

"Marshal, how would you describe Emile's demeanor? Was he hysterical? Did he show anger? Did he appear afraid?"

Stutes shook his head. "I don't know which was calmer, Hebert or the dead winds of the storm that passed. He didn't speak a word or show any emotion. His silence spooked me."

"And what about the weapon, Marshal? Did you find the gun that Emile used in the killing?"

"The gun could not to be found. We did discover that the horse and buggy had been freshly cleaned, and we found muddy clothes soaking in the horse trough."

Prodding, Ogden asked, "And what happened next, Marshal?"

"After making the arrest, we started toward the jail in Lafayette. On our way there, we came upon Victor Hebert on horseback. Presumably, he was heading into the city. He identified Emile as his son, and we drove into the city to confine the prisoner."

"Marshal, did Emile Hebert later confess to shooting Austin Landry, and did he also confess to shooting Sheriff Felix Latiolais and Jules Broussard?"

"Yes, upon arrival at the jail, he confessed to both shootings. He also confessed to tossing the weapon in a field."

"And had you gotten word by then that Austin Landry had died from the gunshot wounds, and was this said to Emile?"

"Yes, we told him that Mr. Landry died about an hour after he was taken to the office of Dr. R. K. Comeaux for care."

"And Marshal, upon hearing of the death of Mr. Landry, did Emile show any grief or express any remorse for the victim?"

Again, Stutes shook his head. "None whatsoever."

"And did you eventually find the murder weapon, Marshal?"

"Yes. Later, when we went to question Charley Harrison, a friend of Hebert, he said that Emile had gone to see him after the killing. We learned that Charley Harrison had gone into the field and fetched the shotgun. He gave it to the deputy."

"And how did Charley know where the murder weapon was?"

"Apparently, when Emile went to see Charley after the killing, he told Charley that he had thrown the gun in a field about a mile from where the shootings took place. Charley went and fetched the gun when the sun came up."

Holding the alleged murder weapon in his hand, Ogden asked, "Is this the weapon Charley Harrison gave to the deputy?"

"Yes, it is. A Winchester 12-gauge pump shotgun."

"Your Honor, the state would like to admit this weapon as Exhibit A."

"Exhibit A is admitted into evidence," replied the judge.

"We have no more questions of the witness, Your Honor."

"Mr. Kennedy, you may proceed."

Kennedy then stood up and turned to the witness stand. "Marshal, you said that you arrived at Emile's farm at five o'clock in the morning. Do you know approximately what time the shootings occurred?"

"According to statements by Emile and witnesses, the shootings happened around eleven o'clock the night before."

"So, would you say that in the six hours that lapsed before you arrived, the defendant had time and opportunity to flee instead of returning to his home?"

Stutes shrugged. "I suppose he could have run if he wanted to."

"Marshal, would you not also say that this type of behavior, that of telling another person where you hid the murder weapon and then quietly going home, is somewhat unusual of someone who has committed the crime of murder in a malicious way?"

"Objection, Your Honor," Ogden interjected. "The question is leading the witness and has no relevance."

"Objection sustained."

Kennedy continued, "Well, then, in your interrogation of the accused after his arrest, did you or anyone else ask Emile why he tossed the gun and why he later told Charley Harrison where the gun could be found?"

"To my recollection and knowledge . . . no."

"And Marshal, in your interrogation of the accused after his arrest, did you or anyone else ask Emile why he didn't run or why he calmly went home, put his wife and child to bed, and went to the barn to clean the horse and buggy and wash the muddy clothes?"

"To my recollection and knowledge . . . no."

"No further questions."

"Redirect, Mr. Ogden?"

"No, Your Honor, the prosecution rests."

"You may step down, Marshal. Mr. Kennedy, is the defense ready?"

"Yes, Your Honor, the defense calls Charley Harrison as our first witness."

Charley Harrison walked to the witness stand and was sworn in.

"Mr. Harrison, is it true that you are Emile's best friend and that he went to see you the night of the incident that occurred near Sugar Mill Road?"

"Yassa, Yassa. I know Emile all my life. We was in the war together and came home. Me and John and others help him work his sugar field. Yassa, Emile come to see me that night." Harrison spoke with his head down, looking up only occasionally, as if searching for words or the confidence to speak them.

In a softer tone, Kennedy continued. "Mr. Harrison, tell us what happened that night when Emile came to see you."

"The night was Tuesday, near midnight. I was sleeping and heard loud sounds, like drums. I went to the door and saw Emile standing, him and Leona and the baby. They was covered in mud, all of them. Emile said he met men walking on the road, Sheriff Felix and others. He said the men told him to get down and help push the car. Emile said he told them no, and they threatened to whip him, so he raised his shotgun to warn. Then, one of them threw a spade and knocked Leona and the baby to the road. Emile said he shot, then the sheriff shot, then he shot again, and the sheriff fell. He said two other men were down."

"Mr. Harrison, you said that Emile told you that when the men threatened to take him down off the buggy, he raised his gun to warn them. Is that what he told you?"

Harrison nodded vigorously, "Yassa."

"And you also said that Emile told you that one of the men threw a spade and knocked Leona and the baby out of the buggy, and then Emile fired the first shot. Is that what Emile told you?"

"Yassa."

"And he also told you that he fired the second shot after the sheriff shot, is that correct?"

"Yassa."

"And did Emile tell you anything about the weapon he used?"

"Yassa. He said he threw the gun in the field a mile back, where the road forked. At sunup, I went to the field and fetched it. When deputies came, I gave them the gun I fetched." Harrison leaned forward in his seat. "That's all I know, suh . . . God's truth."

"Mr. Harrison," Kennedy said, his tone serious, though with a pleading expression on his face, "please look me in the eyes when you answer this question. It is very important. Do you have any idea why Emile knocked on your door that night, and why he told you where he had thrown the gun?"

Harrison raised his head and looked Kennedy in the eyes. "Well, suh, he knocked to tell me what happened, and he said if they found him with the gun, they would kill him. He wanted me to go fetch the gun and give it to the marshal."

"Objection, Your Honor," said Ogden. "This whole line of questioning is hearsay."

"Borderline perhaps, but I'll allow it," stated the judge. "Objection overruled. Tread carefully, Mr. Kennedy. You may proceed."

"Mr. Harrison, earlier you said that you and Emile served in the war together. Are you referring to the Great War?"

"Yassa, we even went to France together. I remember the day we left. They had took us to New York City, and we got on a ship. It was a Sunday, August 25th, 1918."

"And in what infantry did you and Emile serve?"

"82nd Division, 325th Regiment, Company B, suh."

"And did you or Emile come home with a medal for having bravely fought in the war?"

"Emile did, the Croix de Guerre. Not many given to colored soldiers."

"Thank you, Mr. Harrison," Kennedy said, returning to his gentle tone. "I have no further questions."

"Mr. Ogden, your witness." As in his redirect questioning of Raymond Broussard, Ogden stood near his chair and did not approach the witness stand.

"Thank you, Your Honor. Charley, while serving in the military and fighting overseas, I assume that you and Emile were trained in the use of firearms. Is that correct?"

"Yassa, in the fight we carried a 12-gauge pump."

"Was it a 12-gauge pump similar to the one you fetched from the field?"

"Yassa, just like it. Emile bought one for the hunt. He never miss a shot. He could hit a rabbit blindfold."

"Thank you, Charley. I have no further questions."

"Mr. Kennedy, do you wish to redirect?"

"No, Your Honor."

"Very well. You may go, Mr. Harrison. The defense may proceed."

Sidney Roos rose to call another defense witness. "Your Honor, we call the defendant's father, Victor Hebert."

Victor Hebert walked to the witness stand and was sworn in. Roos stood and began his questioning as he stepped toward the witness stand. "Mr. Hebert, you are the father of Emile Hebert, are you not?"

"I am, *oui*."

"Mr. Hebert, did you see Emile the day of the shooting, before the incident?"

"*Oui*. He and Leona come to visit and help in the field. Then the storm come, and they waited while the rain passed."

"Mr. Hebert, when did you learn that your son had been arrested?"

"I was feeding my hogs one morning before the sun come up. I was half-dressed and barefoot. The mayor and the marshal and two deputies drive up. The marshal asked if I seen Emile the day before. I said, '*oui*, Emile and Leona come to visit and waited until the rain let up.' I ask why he wanted to know, but he said nothing and drove off. Then later, Jean, a neighbor not far, come by and said that Emile had been arrested for shooting a man and that he shot the sheriff. He said that Leona and John was arrested, too. I wasted no time and saddled my horse to go to the jail. As I was heading to town, I met the men again, many more this time. They drove up behind me, and they had Emile, Leona, John, and the baby, and was taking them to jail. They asked me the same question about Emile coming to visit the day before, and I answered. Then, they pointed to Emile in the car and asked if he was my son. I said, '*oui*, that's my son Emile.'"

"So, you say they questioned you about Emile's whereabouts twice, once when they went to your home to see you and again when they met you while you were on your horse heading toward the Lafayette jail? Correct?"

"*Oui*. I told them the same, that Emile and Leona come to visit. The storm was bad, so they left late, after dark."

"Mr. Hebert, would you tell the court again what your reaction was when your neighbor Jean told you that Emile had been arrested for shooting a man and the sheriff?"

"I knew it was a lie. Of my eight sons, Emile speak his mind, but he would never shoot a man unless he had to."

"You mean unless it was in self-defense?"

"*Oui*. Emile and John both went to the Great War. They killed men, then. In the bird or the rabbit hunt, Emile is the best shot, but he would never shoot a man unless he had to. Every man here know me and my sons. For some, we built the field and the crop. *Mo lé gason pas asasen.* My sons are not killers."

As if to emphasize the point, Roos asked again, "Mr. Hebert, would you say one more time what you did when you learned that Emile and John had been arrested?"

"And Leona, too. They put Leona and John and the baby in jail. I got on my horse barefoot to go get them. When I got to the jail, I told them to let my children go. *Mo té connain bourreau vini tale.* I knew the hangmen would soon come."

"By the hangmen, do you mean the Ku Klux Klan?"

"*Oui*. I know they would come. We know them. Me and my boys don't fear them. *Jamain nouzot ote chapeau pou yé.* We never tip the hat to them."

"I have no further questions, Mr. Hebert."

"Mr. Ogden?" asked Judge Campbell.

"We have no questions of the witness, Your Honor."

"You may step down, Mr. Hebert. At this time, the court will adjourn until tomorrow," said Judge Campbell as he sounded the gavel to end the day's proceedings.

*Emile Hebert in his
World War I uniform*

John (left) *and Victor Hebert* (right),
the day before John left for WWI

Emile Hebert

Leona Hebert

CHAPTER SEVEN

T he trial resumed on the morning of Wednesday, October 25th. By then, the storm had passed, and the clear skies drew a larger crowd inside and outside of the courthouse. The bailiff reopened the court as Judge Campbell entered the room.

"Good morning. The defense may continue with its witnesses."

"Your Honor," said Roos, standing, "the defense calls the defendant's wife, Leona Hebert."

Wearing a small, brown hat and white dress, the twenty-one-year-old wife of Emile Hebert gave her baby to her father-in-law and stepped toward the witness stand with poise. Leona knew that she was the only person other than her husband who experienced the trauma and horror of that night as he would tell it, horror that still haunted her. She would be plagued with nightmares for the rest of her life. She dreaded the thought of a mob lynching Emile, of not having him by her side, and of Lloyd growing up without a father. As much as she prayed for a not guilty verdict and Emile coming home, the sight of him sitting there, shackled in a courtroom of mostly white people—with white lawyers, a white judge, and white men in the jury box—pushed her into a deep well of pessimism and sorrow. She took the oath, sat down, and looked at Emile, then covered her face and cried. Roos reached into his pocket, gave her a handkerchief, and waited several minutes for her to gain her composure before asking the first question.

"Mrs. Hebert, Sheriff Latiolais and Mr. Broussard both testified that your husband Emile fired his shotgun at the men on the road without giving them a warning. They further testified that the sheriff threw a spade at the buggy after this first shot was fired. Would you say those statements are true or false?"

"False, suh," she replied slowly, recovering from her tears. "They told Emile to get down and come help. Emile said he needed to take us home. He didn't want no trouble."

"And what happened next?"

More composed, but feeling uncomfortable saying the actual words exchanged between the sheriff and Emile, Leona paused. She glanced at the sheriff for a moment, then looked at Emile. "Then they cussed and said they would beat him, and Emile cussed back."

"And did Emile warn the men in any way?"

"He raised the shotgun and pointed, then the sheriff threw the iron."

"And this iron that the sheriff threw, did it hit you or your son, Lloyd?"

"Yessa. The iron cut me here in the head and I fell off the buggy," said Leona, sniffling and wiping tears from her eyes again before pointing to a scar on her forehead.

"And Mrs. Hebert, was your son Lloyd still in your arms when you fell off the buggy onto the ground?"

"Yessa, and he started crying."

"And would you tell the court what happened when you fell to the ground with the baby?"

"When I fell, the buggy wheel rolled over my leg and I screamed."

Leona began to cry harder. Roos again waited a minute before resuming the questioning. From his seat, John Kennedy watched the jury intently. Although the jury showed no reaction, he didn't doubt that Leona's emotional pain was felt. There was complete stillness among those seated in the courtroom. Roos continued. "Mrs. Hebert, did you see or hear gunshots while you were on the ground?"

"I heard shots, but I . . . I didn't see," Leona said, touching the handkerchief to her eyes again.

"No more questions, Your Honor."

Judge Campbell glanced over to the prosecutor and gave a nod, "Mr. Ogden, your witness."

"We have no questions for the witness, Your Honor."

"Very well. You may return to your seat, Mrs. Hebert," responded the judge, delicately.

As Roos took his seat, Kennedy stood and moved toward the jury. "Your Honor, the defense calls the defendant, Emile Hebert, to the stand." The courtroom crowd murmured loudly. Shouts of "Hang him!" and "Hang the nigger!" were heard from the rear, right side of the room.

Slamming his gavel several times, Judge Campbell issue a stern warning, "I will not tolerate any further outburst of that sort in this court."

Other than several jurymen adjusting their posture to sit up straight, none of the twelve men showed any visible reaction to Emile being called to testify.

Escorted by two deputies, Emile Hebert walked slowly to the witness stand and was sworn in. Emile knew that his fate dangled in a web-like thread of truth that some men would see and some would not. He had fought in a war, seen death, and come close to dying himself. But now the enemy was his own government and he was its prisoner. In spirit and conviction, he was still a fighting soldier, but he was without a gun and without men around him whom he could trust. He wanted to live, but he had resolved to die if that was the price of honor and dignity. As he sat and looked at Leona, she again broke down in tears.

Kennedy began, "Emile, please tell the court what happened on the night of June 20th, near Sugar Mill Road."

"Suh, I didn't mean to hurt or kill no one," Emile recounted solemnly. "Me and Leona had went to visit Poppa near Youngsville. We had heavy rain from the storm, and we waited while it passed. When we left, we saw no stars or moon. The mud was boot-high and the buggy barely rolled. My horse pushed back on the crack of the whip. Not far from the cane mill, we met men walking, Sheriff Latiolais and three others. They said the car was trapped in the mud and they told me to let go the buggy to help. I said no. Then they threatened to take me down, so I raised my barrel to warn. One of them threw a spade and hit Leona and the baby, and they fell to the ground. Then, the horse bucked, and the buggy rolled over them. I shot, not knowing where the buckshot fell. One of them went down. The sheriff fired his handgun, but my second round hit him, and he fell. I saw a third man down when I cracked my whip."

"Emile, did you know that one of the men on the road was the sheriff of Lafayette Parish, and did you know any of the other men you met on the road that night?"

"I seen the sheriff many times. I knew who he was. I seen Raymond Broussard, too, but not the others."

"And when you first met the men on the road, did you demand the right-of-way? Did you tell the men to get out of the way and let you pass?"

Emile leaned forward in the witness chair and continued to speak softly and calmly, showing no change of facial expression. "Yessa. I told them that they were in the way. I needed to pass. Then the sheriff told me to get down off the buggy and help them push the car."

"And you said that when they told you to get down and go help with the car, you refused. Why did you refuse to help?"

"It was late. We had the baby. We just wanted home. We didn't want no trouble."

"And how exactly did you answer them? Did you shout or curse or yell obscenities?"

"I said, 'Please, it's late. Leona and the baby need rest. I need to pass.'"

Kennedy walked away from the stand then, as if contemplating the sequence of events. "So, your concern at that point was for Leona and the baby, because it was so late at night, and you had a long ride ahead of you, and you wanted to get them home. Is that correct?"

"Yessa."

"Emile, you said the men threatened to take you down. Do you recall the words they spoke to you?"

After a pause, Emile spoke. "Sheriff Felix cussed and called me a dirty, stinking nigger. He said, 'If you don't come down, I'll whip you so they won't know you.' The others cussed, too."

"And then what happened?"

"Then they came toward the buggy, and I reached for my barrel and raised it."

"And did you say anything when you raised the gun?"

"I said, 'I need to pass. I don't want no trouble.'"

"And had you pumped the gun and cocked the hammer at that point?"

"Nosa, I only raised the barrel."

Turning back toward the witness stand, Kennedy asked, "Emile, can you describe for the court what you were feeling and thinking when you did pull the trigger and pump the first shot? Why did you shoot?"

"It was four to one. They threatened to beat me. When they threw the spade and Leona fell, I thought to shoot, but I didn't. Then the horse bucked, and the wagon rolled, and Leona screamed from below. I stood and the trigger rolled in my hand, and I pulled and let go the pump. When I saw the sheriff reach for his handgun, I released the pump again."

"Did Leona and Lloyd suffer any injuries when they fell and the wagon rolled over them?"

Emile looked at Leona, who was nervously rocking her baby from side to side. "Leona got a cut on the head."

"So, you feared that, because of the hostility the men had already shown and because you were outnumbered four to one—you feared that they would overtake you and do serious harm to you and your family. Is that correct?"

"Yessa."

"Emile, what were you trying to do when you fired the gun?"

Still looking at Leona, Emile replied, "I was trying to stop them so I could get my wife and baby home."

"And what did you do after the shooting?" asked Kennedy, turning to pace again.

"I got down and took Leona and Lloyd out of the mud, and I went down the road and tossed the gun in a field. Then, I went to Charley and told him where it was. I went home and cleaned the horse and buggy and the clothes. Then the marshal came with the posse."

"Emile, would you tell the court why, after tossing the gun, you went to see Charley Harrison and told him where to find it?"

"I tossed the gun 'cuz I knew they would kill me if I had a gun when they came for me. I wanted him to fetch it and turn it in."

"And why didn't you run, Emile? Why did you go home knowing you'd be arrested?"

"I did no wrong. I only did a right. I'm not afraid of the truth."

"Emile, not long after you were incarcerated at the Lafayette Parish jail, you were moved to the St. Mary Parish jail in Franklin, were you not?"

"Yessa."

"Do you know why you were moved? If so, would you tell the court why?"

From his chair, Percy Ogden yelled, "Objection, Your Honor. This line of questioning has no relevance."

"Overruled," said the judge. "Please respond, Mr. Hebert."

"Men come that night and try and take me out to hang me."

"Emile, were there ever any incidents prior to the shooting in which men threatened to hang you?"

Again, Ogden quickly responded, "Objection, Your Honor."

"Overruled. Witness may answer the question."

"Yessa, I met men on the road one night. They said my day was coming 'cuz I don't tip the hat . . . I don't show respect. That's why I carry the barrel in the buggy."

"And when you met those men on the road, were they wearing plain clothes with their heads uncovered or were they wearing hoods?"

"They had hoods."

"Thank you, Emile. No further questions, Your Honor."

"Your witness, Mr. Ogden," said Judge Campbell.

Rising, Ogden paused, and then began his questioning. "Mr. Hebert, in the testimony you gave just minutes ago, you were asked how you answered the men when you refused to move off the road. You were specifically asked if you shouted and cursed. And you said that you spoke politely. We also heard the testimony of your wife, in which she said that you cussed after the men threatened you. Which is it, Mr. Hebert? Did you cuss, or did you not cuss? Whose lie are we supposed to believe . . . yours or your wife's?"

Kennedy jumped from his seat. "Objection, Your Honor. He's badgering."

"Overruled. Answer the question, Mr. Hebert."

"I cussed when they threatened to take me down."

"And so now your story changes," said Ogden, smiling and looking at the jury. "Well, here's a story that I'm sure hasn't changed. Did you confess to killing Austin P. Landry?"

"Yessa."

"And did you also confess to firing a second shot that seriously wounded Sheriff Felix Latiolais and Jules Broussard?"

"Yessa."

Walking up to Emile, Ogden asked, "Mr. Hebert, had any of the men you met on the road that night pulled a gun or threatened to shoot or kill you before you stood up in the buggy and pumped a shot at Austin Landry?"

"They said they would take me down and beat me and they threw a spade."

"That's not what I asked you," said Ogden, with his voice rising as he slammed his fist on the rail of the witness stand. "I asked you if before you stood up and pumped a shot into the chest of Austin Landry, did any of those men point a gun at you or threaten to shoot or kill you?"

Understanding Ogden's objective, Emile forced himself to react calmly to the hostility in the prosecutor's tone and questions. He had seen it before, when the marshal arrested and interrogated him after the shooting, and in the deputies' treatment of him in the four months that he had been in jail. As in those moments, he now clung to the singular thread of the fabric of himself that set him apart from those men, the one thing that enabled him to calmly surrender after the shooting. He clung to his sense of right and wrong, believing that regardless of the trial's outcome, he did no wrong in protecting his wife and child. As a prisoner of injustice, it was the only weapon he had to defend himself.

"Nosa," Emile responded, looking Ogden steadily in the eye.

"And so, neither of the men drew a gun. Neither of them said they would shoot or kill you. But, because you were afraid or you got angry, you took justice and the lives of those men into your own hands."

Once again, Kennedy called out to the judge, "Objection!"

"Sustained."

Stepping away from the stand, Ogden changed tactics. "Mr. Hebert, yesterday, Charley Harrison testified that you were trained in the use of a 12-gauge pump shotgun while serving in the military. And both Charley and your father, Victor, testified that you are always the best shooter on a rabbit hunt. So, are we right to assume that you are an expert marksman in the use of this firearm?"

"Objection, Your Honor!" replied Kennedy, now nearly shouting himself.

"I withdraw the question," said Ogden. "Mr. Hebert, since neither of the men drew a gun before you stood over them with a 12-gauge pump shotgun, could you have made the choice not to shoot . . . even after you supposedly warned them and even though, according to your story, the spade was thrown and Leona and the baby fell off the wagon? Seeing that these men had not made an actual threat to shoot or kill you, could you have chosen not to shoot?"

"Nosa."

Ogden again moved closer to Hebert and the pitch of his voice got louder. "Then why, Emile? Since you felt so compelled to fire your shotgun, why in God's name did you, knowing that you were the only person on that road who was holding a gun in his hand . . . why in God's name did you not fire that gun at the muddy ground or the trees or the stars?

Why did you point your barrel at an unarmed man and pump lead into his heart?"

"Objection, Your Honor. He's badgering the witness," Kennedy shouted.

"Overruled. Please answer the question, Mr. Hebert."

"They hit Leona and Lloyd with the spade and made them fall under the wheel."

"And so, because, as you say, Sheriff Latiolais threw a spade that caused Leona and the baby to fall off the wagon, and because a horse bucked a little and caused the wheel to roll over Leona, did that justify your unloading a 12-gauge pump shotgun on four men who had drawn no weapon on you? Did that justify murder?"

"Yessa."

"No further questions, Your Honor," said Ogden, returning to his seat.

"Redirect, Mr. Kennedy?"

"Yes, Your Honor," said Kennedy, rising and stepping toward the witness stand. "Emile, let's continue the prosecutor's line of questioning, but not in his words. Tell us in your words. Tell the court, first of all, who was the first to show hostility and violent behavior, you or the men you met on the road?"

"They did, suh. They threatened to beat me. Then, they hit my wife in the head with the spade and knocked her and my son on the ground."

"And tell the court why the words and actions of those men justified the outcome. Why did your fear and anger justify your shooting those men? Why, in your heart, do you feel you were right to shoot?"

"We bothered no one. We only wanted home. I didn't mean to kill or hurt no one. I didn't shoot to kill. I shot to stop them. I shot for my wife and child."

"Thank you, Emile. Your Honor, the defense rests."

"Mr. Ogden, do you wish to present any rebuttal questions?"

"No, Your Honor."

"Very well. Bailiff, please escort the accused to his seat. Because of the lateness of the hour, I would like to go directly to closing arguments and then recess for the day. This will give the jury the remainder of the evening to deliberate. Mr. Ogden, are you prepared to give your first closing statement?"

Ogden thanked Judge Campbell before stepping toward the jury.

"Gentlemen, I'm going to be brief, because the law is so clear and the evidence presented is so compelling that I needn't speak long. I needn't argue what the defense has failed to show. You have seen and heard it yourselves. The defense's failure to show convincing justification for the shooting and to defend Hebert's murderous act is as clear as the blue sky that burst through the clouds when the rains ended earlier today. What is clear, gentlemen, is that a good man is dead, and Emile Hebert confessed to killing him—I repeat—confessed to killing him, a confession in which Hebert described how he stood up in his buggy that bloody evening and rained gunshots down on a party of four men. What is clear is Hebert's admission that the weapon used in the killing, and which was later found after he tossed the gun into a field, was his weapon, one that he was highly trained to fire accurately. What is clear, gentlemen, is that the shooting was not an accident and not in self-defense.

"Finally, gentlemen, what is as clear as the voice that you hear me speaking now is that not one of those men, not a single one of them, pointed a gun at Emile Hebert and threatened to shoot him. None of those men provoked Emile Hebert to stand up in that buggy and blast pellets at them. None of them said to Hebert, 'Get down from that buggy or I'll kill you.' Even if he felt threatened, would that be cause to fire a deadly weapon on four men at close range?

"Absolutely not. Gentlemen, the testimony you have heard leaves not even a shadow of doubt that Emile Hebert fired that gun with the willful intent to take not just one life but four," said Ogden, pointing toward Emile without looking at him. "Why did Hebert shoot? Was it because he got angry when the sheriff asked him to kindly get down off the buggy and help those men push a stalled car out of a muddy road? Was it because he got angry when the sheriff threw a spade toward the buggy and the horse bucked and caused his wife and child to fall? Did Hebert shoot because he got even angrier when a wagon wheel rolled over his wife's leg?"

Ogden paused and looked at Emile Hebert. Emile didn't look away. Intending to stir some reaction or change the deadpan look on Hebert's face, Ogden moved closer to Hebert while speaking to the jury. "The answer to each of those questions is a resounding yes. Yes, gentlemen, Emile Hebert fired that rifle because he got angry, and, in his anger, he lost all sense of reason, self-control, and respect for human life. In his anger, he decided that he was going to kill the men who stood in his way."

Then, turning to look at the jury, Ogden made the most convincing and damaging point of his argument. "I ask you, gentlemen, who was the first man to aim a weapon? Who was the first to fire a weapon? The first man to aim and fire a gun was the man who coldly and without remorse confessed to the killing."

Again pointing at Hebert while staring into the eyes of the jury, Ogden summed up his closing. "Gentlemen, Emile Hebert shot and killed, not because those men threatened him with a weapon, not because Hebert feared for his life and that of his family. He killed because he was in a fit of rage. All of the testimony and evidence you have heard and seen today proved that beyond any reasonable doubt. Emile Hebert committed murder and he is guilty of it, a shooting that was deliberate and with the specific intent to cause great bodily harm, resulting in the death of an innocent man and the wounding of two others, including the highest-ranking law enforcement officer of this parish. Your duty, gentlemen, is to apply the law and consider the facts and evidence that you've seen and heard, all of which proved Hebert's malicious and willful intent to kill. I implore you to declare this man guilty of murder in the first-degree."

Following Ogden's statement, the murmuring among white and colored people in the audience rose to a rumble, as if they sensed that the prosecution's argument was strong and convincing enough to guarantee a guilty verdict. Judge Campbell hit the gavel twice. Hebert was expressionless. Although most jurymen showed no reaction, several nodded their heads.

As Ogden took his seat, Kennedy rose and walked toward the jurymen. Standing in one place and looking the twelve jurymen squarely in their eyes, Kennedy began his closing statement.

"Distinguished jurymen, surely it would be much to ask you to not see Emile Hebert as a colored man, one of Creole descent, defiant in some ways. But is it much to ask that you see Emile as a man who, just four years ago, fought beside your own sons and brothers, face down in the dirt trenches and green fields of France, to protect our freedom and democracy? Is it much to ask that you see Emile Hebert as a decorated soldier who marched in cadence, decked in olive drab and crown-creased hat, and who proudly and courageously defended our stars and stripes?

"Good men of this jury, this is 1922, not yet winter. Already, forty Negroes have been unlawfully hanged in this country. At least five men, colored and white, have been reported lynched in Louisiana. Some have vanished in broad daylight, never to be seen again. Just two months ago, two white men in Mer Rouge were kidnapped and are still not found. One of them, F. Watt Daniel, fought bravely in the Great War, as did our defendant. The KKK has virtually taken control of north Louisiana. They have now established chapters in our southern region. Many urge Governor John Parker to call on President Harding to intercede and stop the rampage of the invisible empire that terrorizes and spills innocent blood across the sweet soils of our state.

"You might ask, 'What does that have to do with this case and whether Emile Hebert is guilty or innocent?' Well, I'll tell you, gentlemen. The racial climate of the times in which we live have a great deal to do with this case. As most of you are Catholic, you know that some men hate and do harm to others simply because those people are Catholics, Jews, and Negroes. You also know that the victims of these crimes are sometimes able to defend themselves against such attacks. Other times, as in the case of Emile Hebert, the outcome is tragic, and innocence must be decided in a court of law. Our prosecutor wants to see the blood of injustice spilled in this court. He wants to prove guilt of an innocent man and see him hanged. I beg you, gentlemen, in the name of honor and decency, let truth and justice prevail."

Kennedy paused briefly and turned to look at Emile. "Yes, gentlemen, Emile Hebert did fire the shot that killed Austin P. Landry. Yes, Emile did fire the shot that wounded Sheriff Felix Latiolais and Jules Broussard. Yes, Emile did confess to the shooting. But the question is when, gentlemen, when did he shoot, and why did he shoot? He shot when Sheriff Latiolais threatened to harm him. He shot after he warned the sheriff by raising and pointing his shotgun. He shot after the sheriff slung a spade toward him that knocked his wife and baby into the muddy ditch. He shot after the horse bucked, and the wagon moved, and the wheel of the wagon rolled over his wife and baby. Yes, he did shoot in anger, but he shot as any one of you would, because he feared for his life and the lives of his wife and child." This remark caused several members of the jury to look away from Kennedy and look toward Ogden.

Kennedy walked away from the jury, turned to look at the sheriff, and pointed at him. "Emile shot, gentlemen, because our sheriff was wrong and because Emile knew he was on the right side of justice."

Turning back to face the jury, Kennedy lowered the pitch of his voice. "And for that reason, gentlemen, Emile Hebert didn't flee. For that reason, Emile went to see Charley Harrison after the shooting and asked Charley to go and retrieve the murder weapon. For that reason, Emile calmly and quietly went home, cleaned himself up, and surrendered to Marshal Stutes and his posse without resisting arrest. Why? Because in his heart, Emile knew that his conscience was clear—that he was on the right side of justice.

"Gentlemen, I implore you to look beyond the drama and showmanship of our esteemed prosecutor and examine the facts and evidence. More importantly, I urge you to look into the hearts of Emile and Leona Hebert, and, in doing so, search your own. Ask yourselves this. If you believe that Emile and Leona Hebert are decent, honest people, as each of you are, if in your hearts you believe that, with the eyes of Almighty God gazing upon them, Emile and Leona spoke the truth, the whole truth, and nothing but the truth, what would you have done? Would you have done what Emile Hebert did? Would you have shot, not intending to kill, but to love? If a blackbird can defend its nest, why can't a Negro defend his family?"

Kennedy had gone beyond the law, speaking to the hearts of ordinary people, and tapped into their empathy and sense of compassion. He had held up a mirror of humanity for the jury to see itself. A somber mood filled the air. A pin drop could be heard among those seated in the courtroom. Not a whisper or murmur was said. Ogden, who had not smoked during the entire trial, pulled a pack of cigarettes from the side pocket of his coat. Before he lit a cigarette, Kennedy drew to a conclusion.

"Gentlemen, if you know right and wrong, as I believe you do, declare Emile Hebert innocent, set him free and return him to his wife and child."

As Kennedy moved toward his seat, Ogden put the unlit cigarette down, walked to the jury stand, and faced the jurymen.

"As surely as my duty is to prosecute violators of the law, I support Judge Campbell's action to ensure the safety of the prisoner and the preservation of justice. I wholeheartedly support Judge Campbell's decision to keep the peace by bringing militia into this courtyard for the first time in parish history and to search those who enter. I, too, would urge our governor to stop the rampant violent acts of the KKK by whatever means possible. The tyranny must cease."

Raising the pitch of his voice and pointing a finger at Emile, Ogden continued. "But let us be clear. Whether he be Negro or Caucasian, and with due respect to the honorable service the defendant has given our country, Emile Hebert is a confessed murderer. It is Hebert who is on trial here, not the Ku Klux Klan. It is Hebert who created terror and caused innocent blood to be spilled, namely the blood of Austin P. Landry, the red blood that spewed from Austin Landry's arteries into the blackness of a muddy road."

Clearly intending to stir the jurymen's emotions, Ogden, now pacing the floor, shifted attention away from Emile to the deceased victim's family. "And what about the deceased victim's wife and children, awakened from their dreams, not by the city marshal and his posse, but by a nightmare come true . . . the news that their loving, warmhearted husband and father was brutally gunned down . . . and to see him lying stiff on the undertaker's table. Have we no sympathy for them?"

Loud murmuring could now be heard among white members of the audience. Several members of the jury turned to look at each other and slowly moved their heads from side to side.

"Gentlemen, the defense has attempted to establish doubt about the testimony of the witnesses—victims, I might add. They have attempted to establish doubt about when the spade was thrown and when the first shot was fired. They have even tried to discredit and cast aspersion on the integrity of a respected, duly elected official of this parish. They have attempted to divert your attention away from the guilt of the accused to the alleged crimes of the KKK."

In closing, Ogden moved closer to the jurymen, gradually raising his voice to a crescendo. "But is there any doubt that Emile Hebert has confessed to the crimes for which he is being tried? Is there any doubt that Emile Hebert was the first to draw a gun? Is there any doubt that he held in his hands a weapon whose deadly force he was fully aware of? Is there any doubt that if Emile Hebert wanted to give a warning, he could have chosen to fire that weapon at the stars rather than at the heart of Austin Landry? Is there any doubt that he fired that weapon with the full intent to kill Landry and that he fired again with the full intent to kill three other men?

"Gentlemen, the evidence is absolute and convincing. Having heard the true account of what happened that night near Sugar Mill Road, as spoken by Sheriff Felix Latiolais and by Raymond Broussard, both eyewitnesses to the shooting, you now have a duty to rise and render judgment . . .

judgment Hebert justly deserves, that being the verdict of guilty . . . guilty of murder and mass assault of the first-degree. I pray you Godspeed."

Once again, the prosecutor's argument drew whispering murmurs across all sides of the courtroom. Among most white people there, heads turned and nodded, and eyes glanced, as if to say that Ogden had tied the noose and nailed the coffin with his final closing remarks.

"Thank you, gentlemen," said Judge Campbell. "It is now near six o'clock in the evening. The court will recess to allow the jury to deliberate. If they cannot reach an agreement this evening, they will resume proceedings tomorrow morning. For the record, I wish to note that the jury has already been pre-instructed on applicable law and on its duties as jurymen. If necessary, the jury will remain sequestered in quarters behind the courtroom and will deliberate at their free will."

CHAPTER EIGHT

The twelve jurymen, all male and white, walked the long hallway leading to the deliberation room. The room was small but had three large windows with a view of the oak-canopied courtyard at the rear of the courthouse, now lined with tents pitched by National Guardsmen. A large conference table sat in the center.

Most of the jurymen, whose occupations ranged from laborers to business owners, were Catholic. None were over fifty years old. Several, such as Alex Verot and Eraste Landry, two of the area's largest landowners and farmers, were actively engaged in Lafayette civic and business organizations. Fred and P. J. Voorhies, members of a prominent Lafayette family, were business owners. Forty-one-year-old L. P. DeBlanc, the jury foreman, had organized one of the first major banks of Lafayette and was active in the local homebuilders association.

Verot and Landry took seats at the table. Fred and P. J. Voorhies entered next. Fred walked in slowly, hands in his pockets, while P. J. poured himself a glass of water from a pitcher on the table. The other jurymen ambled in and stood around the table or wandered around the room before sitting.

The weather was unseasonably warm for late October. DeBlanc opened the windows and remained standing. "Gentlemen," said DeBlanc, "we've been given our instructions, and you've heard the testimony and seen the evidence. I guess a good place to start would be a vote on Hebert's guilt or innocence. Would you rather we do that by ballot or openly?"

Even at the start of the meeting, it was apparent that several jurymen had already decided on Emile's guilt or innocence. One such jury member was Walter Block.

"Makes me no difference," said Block. "I vote guilty. No question about it. Hebert gave those men no warning. He shot and killed, and he confessed to doing it."

"But according to him and his wife, he did warn, and he acted in self-defense," said Lot Tarver, speaking up for the less-decided jurymen.

"And the sheriff threatened to beat Hebert. That's when he raised his gun to warn them. Then the sheriff threw a spade that hurt the wife and baby. Hebert didn't shoot until he heard his wife scream beneath the wheel of the wagon," said DeBlanc.

"Well, that's their story," said Luc Langlinais, chuckling. "But Sheriff Latiolais and Raymond Broussard say differently. They said Hebert fired before the sheriff threw the spade. Somebody's lying. I'm inclined to side with the sheriff."

"Look, I voted for Latiolais, and he's given this parish good service," said Lot Tarver. "But let's face it. He's used that badge and pistol to intimidate and bully a lot of people, colored and white. I've yet to meet a politician who won't lie to save his ass. They all do."

"Let's keep it going. Let's hear what everybody's got to say," said DeBlanc. "Eraste, what do you think?"

"A good man is dead, and two others are wounded. To be honest, I don't know who's lying, Latiolais and Broussard or Hebert and his wife. But I find it strange that Hebert went to see Harrison, told him where the gun was, and didn't run. He went home, knowing he'd be arrested, maybe hanged. That doesn't sound like the behavior of a so-called madman. I'm on the fence."

"I agree," said Fred Voorhies. "We've got two witnesses to the crime telling one story and two witnesses saying just the opposite. Quite honestly, I don't think Ogden made the case that Hebert shot maliciously. I'm in doubt—a dark shadow of doubt, I might add."

Ivy Tarver, the youngest member of the jury at age thirty-four, had been pacing the floor and smoking a cigarette. "Well, I'm not," he said, raising his voice while pointing his cigarette at Fred Voorhies. "Like Ogden said, Hebert could have shot in the air if he wanted to give a warning. Instead, he shot directly at those men. Makes perfect sense to me. You don't warn somebody who is unarmed by shooting at them."

"But Hebert said that he didn't shoot until Latiolais threw the spade and hit the wife," said P. J. Voorhies. "Even then, Hebert didn't shoot. He shot when the horse bucked, and the wagon rolled over the wife."

"Well, like Luc said, that's his story," said Alex Verot, "but, even then, he could have shot into the air, as Ivy said. The only other armed man was the sheriff, and he didn't shoot until Hebert shot. Hebert just got angry, lost his temper, and got out of control. At the least, he should get second-degree. He did commit—and confessed to—murder."

"I agree. I think any man who admits to committing murder, self-defense or not, has committed murder," said Lenox Hoffpauir. "He is clearly guilty of it. It's just a question of degree."

"I don't know Hebert, but based upon what I heard, I find it hard to believe that he is the kind of young man who'd shoot anybody maliciously," said C. McDonald. "He's a war veteran. I think he found himself at war and shot to defend himself. Like he said, he was outnumbered four to one."

"I agree with Eraste and Fred," said P. J. Voorhies. "Both sides are convincing but somebody's lying. I just didn't hear enough from either side to erase doubt as to which story is the truth. Isn't that what the prosecutor is supposed to do to secure a conviction?"

"I'm leaning strongly toward guilty," said Leonard Bourgeois. "Even if Hebert only warned by pointing his gun, he clearly put the sheriff and those men on the defense at that point. The sheriff could have dropped the spade and pulled his revolver when Hebert raised his shotgun, but he threw the spade instead. Hebert just got angry when he heard his wife scream below the wheel. It was anger that caused him to shoot, not self-defense."

"And him being a veteran only hurts his case," said Hoffpauir. "Hebert knew the power of that weapon, and he was good at shooting it. Even his daddy said it. He shot to kill, not to defend himself. But even if it was in self-defense, the man killed and confessed to doing it. He ain't innocent by any means."

Visibly upset by what he had heard several jurors say, Eraste Landry slammed his fist on the table and stood up. "Well, damn it, I'd get angry, too, if someone threatened to whip my ass and then knocked my wife and baby to the muddy ground with an iron rod!"

"But did that justify Hebert unloading his gun to kill four men . . . him getting pissed off?" asked Block. "The sheriff mentioned the hot temper of the Hebert boys. That's why the marshal arrested Emile's brother. He probably would have gone into town and shot the first white man he saw."

"Was that reason to kill?" answered McDonald. "No. But what troubles me is Ogden and the sheriff painting this man to be some kind of devil, when all he was doing was trying to protect his wife and child. If anybody's guilty of a crime, I'd say it's the sheriff. He lied and he did it after swearing to tell the truth with his hand on the Bible."

"But it's not just a question of anger," said P. J. Voorhies, also rising to stand and look down on the men seated. "Eraste makes a good point.

The man was scared for his life and the life of his wife and child. As far as he knew, his wife and baby could have been very seriously injured, hurt enough to be dying below the wheel of that wagon. I just don't think we have seen and heard enough to say that Hebert acted maliciously and with intent to kill those men. And I also don't think that we heard enough to say that he didn't. Ogden just failed to make the case."

"Of all the testimony I heard," said Langlinais, "I think the marshal's testimony sealed it for me. If Hebert killed in self-defense, you would think that he would have showed some remorse after hearing that Landry had died. But he didn't."

"But he did say on the witness stand that he didn't mean to harm anyone," said Landry. "The man just wanted to get his wife and baby home. It was after eleven o'clock at night, for God's sake."

"What I'm really troubled by is the possibility that Latiolais could have lied," said Fred Voorhies. "I wouldn't want it on my conscience that we had a man executed because the sheriff lied. If Hebert is to be hanged, there has to be no doubt that he shot maliciously with the intent to kill. I have serious doubt as to whether Latiolais's story is truthful. Broussard's, too, for that matter."

After taking a vote, DeBlanc counted half the jurymen in favor of a guilty verdict and half who were either in favor of an acquittal or simply could not decide guilt or innocence. The deliberation continued for another hour.

CHAPTER NINE

By eight o'clock the following morning, the courtroom was standing room only. No one inside said a word. The local newspaper had covered each day of the trial, and the presence of the National Guard created a spectacle that many residents of the parish, white and colored, couldn't resist witnessing. Hundreds stood on the grounds awaiting the jury's decision. At 9:00 a.m., as the bright rays of the morning sun burst through the large windows of the courtroom, the bailiff entered and opened the trial.

"Mr. DeBlanc, it is my understanding that the jury has reached a decision," said Judge Campbell.

Foreman DeBlanc stood to read the jury's decision. "Yes, Your Honor. We have."

"Very well. Emile Hebert, please stand and face the jury while the verdict is read."

The entire courtroom held their breaths. Leona bent down, bowed her head, and hid her face in her hands. Emile stood and faced the twelve men who had decided whether he would be lynched, set free, or spend the rest of his life in prison. His gaze was stoic and stone-like. Standing steadfast as a soldier, the past and his future suddenly flashed. He saw men in the middle of a muddy road. He saw a hurling shovel and the horse bucking. He heard Leona screaming on the ground and felt a trigger rolling in his hand. The gun blasts of his rifle rang in his ears. The seconds before the jury foreman spoke were an eternity. Emile saw heaven and tasted the bitter, salty earth.

"Your Honor, as you know, we are farmers, storekeepers, and laborers of industry, some learned, some not, but all cherish the sovereignty of property and the comfort of order. I believe I speak for every juryman. None of us condones violence or the violation of rights, be they property or human. But neither can we condone the abuse of power or the partial execution of law. Yesterday, we were taken to our quarters shortly after sundown. After much deliberation, we can only conclude that our collective sense cannot distinguish between twilight and night. There is law, and there is justice. We find it impossible in this case to reconcile them. Final judgment might best be left to means beyond our bounds of reason. We leave that to the makers and interpreters of law to decide.

"We believe that what happened that night near Sugar Mill Road was a duel, not of firearms, but of principles. We can discern neither truth nor falsehood in the words spoken during the trial. Therefore, we the jury are not able to reach a verdict. We cannot conclude that Emile Hebert is innocent or guilty of the State's charges. And that is the final decision of most jurymen."

When the foreman ended his statement, the courtroom erupted with shouts of anger and jubilation. Colored people in the rear were the most exuberant, shaking hands, jumping with joy, and hugging each other. Judge Campbell slammed his gavel repeatedly. Kennedy, Roos, Leona, and Victor joyfully embraced. With hands and feet shackled, Emile looked at them blankly as if he had not fully processed the jury's decision and what it meant. Kennedy and Roos had counseled him about a mistrial being a possible, but unlikely, outcome. He knew that he was still not free, and even if he were, he would be a hunted man for as long as he lived. Leona, smiling with tears of joy streaming down her cheeks, raised a hand of their three-month-old son Lloyd to wave to his father. Emile smiled then bowed his head.

"Order! Order! Order in this courtroom," said Judge Campbell while continuing to slam his gavel. "Well, a surprising verdict indeed, but then, not so surprising in light of the case that has been presented and the testimony we have heard here. Having heard the jury foreman's most eloquent statement, I hereby declare this a mistrial. The eight men of the pool list are free to return home. The four regular jurymen shall remain for further service to the court. I am deeply indebted to the National Guardsmen of New Iberia and Lafayette for the order they have kept in this most trying circumstance. They, too, are free to return to their homes and families. Thank you, gentlemen, for your service.

"This case is now remanded back to the State to decide whether it will retry the accused. In the meantime, the prisoner shall remain shackled and in custody pending my decision later today to set bail. Deputies, kindly escort the prisoner. This court is adjourned."

———

Speaking at a press conference several months after the trial, Governor Parker was questioned about the Hebert case.

"Well, Governor, what about Emile Hebert, the Negro who was tried for murder a few months ago in Lafayette Parish?" one reporter asked. "Rumor has it that the DA is considering retrying the case. Will you again order the National Guard to be present during the trial?"

"I will only say this," Parker responded, pausing briefly, "for all those men . . . Emile Hebert, Daniel and Richards in Mer Rouge, *and* the KKK . . . justice will prevail."

———

Shortly after being released on bail, Emile Hebert put his wife on a train to Ames, Texas, where he had relatives. Legend has it that Hebert, fearing that he would be hunted and killed, then disguised himself and caught a ride on a chicken truck. Hiding beneath coops of chickens, Emile took the nearly two-hundred-mile journey from Youngsville to Ames to reunite with his wife and child. The district attorney never sought to retry the case.

Emile and his family lived in constant fear that either the Ku Klux Klan or men who were vengeful of the death of Austin Landry would find and kill him or members of his family. It is said that some family members even changed the spelling or pronunciation of their last name. When the *Southern Consumers Times*, a Black newspaper in Lafayette, published the story of Emile Hebert's trial in the spring of 1984, several members of Hebert's immediate family were extremely upset, not simply because the story had been published, but because it said that Hebert was still alive and noted where he lived. For fear of Emile being hunted and killed, his whereabouts had remained a family secret for more than sixty years.

Emile Hebert never returned to Louisiana, not even for the burials of his parents and siblings. While living in Ames, he acquired twenty-five acres and continued to farm. He died on October 17, 1991, at the age of ninety-five. Of the thirteen children of Victor and Victoire Hebert, he lived the longest.

Emile Hebert (left) *in Ames, Texas*

Epilogue

The KKK had entered southwest Louisiana toward the end of 1921 and established chapters in Crowley, Lafayette, New Iberia, and Opelousas, four of the region's most populated towns. Their chartered membership numbered nearly three hundred. Preaching law, order, and morality, their ranks quickly grew, mostly among Protestants. Yet by the summer of 1923, the Klan's influence in the region had begun to diminish.

Few Louisianans, including members of the Hebert family, know the facts and details of the trial of Emile Hebert. Even fewer know its historical significance in changing the racial climate of Lafayette Parish and in helping Governor John Parker's crusade to end the terror and dominance of the KKK.

Black residents of Lafayette at the time of Hebert's trial later recounted that, after the trial, they saw a marked difference in how white residents treated them. It was said that, prior to Hebert's trial, Black men were frequent victims of whippings and beatings by white men. Few, if any, African American men would dare defy or challenge a white person publicly and escape the brutal consequences. After Hebert's trial, local whites, out of fear, guilt, or enlightenment, did not move as quickly to strike a colored man. Caution, temperance, and sensitivity set in.

No doubt the presence of the National Guard during Hebert's trial, reportedly the first time that the military had been deployed in connection with a trial in Lafayette Parish, prevented Hebert from being unlawfully hanged. In the spring of 1923, less than a year after Hebert's trial, the Lafayette Parish KKK publicly announced its disbandment. The outcome of the trial alone did not definitively cause the eventual decline of the KKK's presence in the parishes of southwest Louisiana. Surely, other circumstances and events, including the Klan's virulent anti-Catholic and anti-Jewish acts and the dominant presence of Catholics in the region, coupled with the negative public backlash to the horrific nature of the Mer Rouge murders, were the strongest contributing factors to the halt of the KKK's march into the region. Still, Hebert's escape from the KKK's noose was clearly a major setback for them at the height of their prominence in that region of the state. If nothing else, it helped to reinforce the intolerance that many of the area's community and religious leaders had for bigotry and racial hatred.

By the end of Hebert's trial in late October of that year, the bodies of the two white men in Morehouse Parish who had spoken out against the Klan had yet to be found. Governor Parker's fight was just beginning.

POSTSCRIPT

The Ku Klux Klan entered Morehouse Parish in late 1921, peddling an elixir of promises to rid the parish of lawlessness, including bootlegging, gambling, and prostitution. Their membership quickly grew, especially in Bastrop, the parish seat, where most, if not all, government officials joined their ranks. In time, their tactics turned to coercion, intimidation, and violence, not only toward those who practiced "immorality" but against anyone who voiced opposition to the KKK.

Whether the Ku Klux Klan was responsible for the kidnapping and killing of Filmore Watt Daniel and Thomas F. Richards, two residents of Morehouse Parish, in the summer of 1922 remains a question. No one was ever convicted. In fact, there was never a trial. Why the KKK would choose to single out those particular men is also left to speculation. It was rumored that the men had been part of an attempted assassination of Dr. B. M. McKoin, a local physician and Klan leader, months before. It was also rumored that McKoin had in fact staged the attempted assassination himself to justify the kidnappings. It was reported that the two men had on several occasions publicly spoken out against the Klan. In the mind of Governor Parker, there wasn't any doubt that the KKK was the culprit. Parker exerted every effort within his power to find the missing men and render justice. He accomplished the former but not the latter.

Daniel was thirty-five years old at the time of his kidnapping. A graduate of Louisiana State University, he had served in World War I as a sergeant in the US Army. He was a farmer, single, and known for being somewhat of a "ladies' man" around Morehouse Parish. He was also fairly indiscriminate in his choice of women's marital status and race. Daniel was described as being intolerant of the KKK and "fearless" of them. His occasional outspokenness directly in the Klan's face was well documented.

Richards was thirty-one years old. He was married with two children and employed as an automobile mechanic. Like Daniel, he was known to have had public confrontations with members of the Klan.

According to testimony by individuals questioned by investigators, Daniel and Richards were last seen on the afternoon of August 24th, following a baseball game and community barbecue that took place in Bastrop, located nine miles from Mer Rouge. The event was held to grow support for a bond issue to build roads and was attended by several hundred residents. One account reported thousands in attendance. Using a pickup truck to block the road from Bastrop to Mer Rouge, a large group of hooded and armed Klansmen stopped and searched every vehicle leaving the event. Daniel, Richards, and three other men, including Daniel's father, were taken from their vehicles, blindfolded, and bound. All but one of the men was badly beaten. Three of them were released. Daniel and Richards were never seen alive again.

On September 5th, a grand jury, mostly comprised of Klan members, was convened in Bastrop to investigate the kidnappings. The case was dismissed. Three or four days later, Governor Parker directed State Attorney General Adolph Coco to initiate an investigation. Parker also offered a $500 reward for information that would lead to the arrest and conviction of persons responsible for the kidnappings. It was later reported that the governor spent his personal money to augment the investigation. He wrote to and personally met with US President Warren G. Harding to get the Federal Bureau of Investigation to come to Louisiana and investigate the kidnappings. Federal investigators came, but soon found themselves similarly intimidated by the KKK. They uncovered no information leading to the whereabouts of the missing men.

On December 19th, Governor Parker declared martial law in Morehouse Parish and sent National Guardsmen to provide protection for divers who had begun searching lakes and bayous for the bodies of Daniel and Richards. Several days later, an explosion occurred in Lake Lafourche near Mer Rouge, bringing the bodies of Daniel and Richards to surface. No one knew who set off the dynamite that caused the explosion, but the mutilated condition of the bodies would suggest that there was more to the crime that any formal investigation could have possibly discovered. An autopsy report concluded that the men had been severely beaten. Their bodies had been crushed by what appeared to be a road grading machine, their legs and arms were missing, and Daniel had been castrated. The only thing that surfaced was the men's torsos. They were identified by what remained of the clothing they wore.

McKoin, who had left the state and gone to Baltimore, was soon arrested at the direction of Governor Parker and charged with the murder of Daniel and Richards. Klan leader Jeff Burnett had already been charged as a suspect in the crime. Parker and Coco convened an open hearing on January 5, 1923, to gather evidence against McKoin, Burnett, and other members of the Klan. Fifty witnesses testified, implicating the KKK. On March 5th, a new grand jury comprised of twelve white jurors was convened in Bastrop to hear testimony and examine evidence related to the kidnappings and murders. After ten days, they reported that there was insufficient evidence to issue an indictment against anyone accused of the crimes. No one was tried and the case was closed.

The horrific nature of the murders in Mer Rouge sparked a national debate on the role of the KKK in American society. From the month that Daniel and Richards disappeared to a year after Governor Parker declared martial law in Morehouse Parish, more than one hundred articles about the Mer Rouge murders appeared in the *New York Times*, many on the front page. In spite of the Klan's rhetoric of patriotism and morality, the public reaction to the Mer Rouge murders and the Klan's presumed connection to them was generally negative, leading to further investigations of Klan activities, the disbandment of the KKK in Morehouse Parish, and a weakening of the KKK's influence in Louisiana and nationally.

Notes & Acknowledgments

I am the oldest grandson of Andrew Hebert, who was ten years old when his brother Emile was tried for murder. I discovered details of the trial in April 1984, when, as a resident of Lafayette, Louisiana, I was doing community economic development work for the city government. One Friday evening after work, I went to the office of Alfred "Mac" McZeal, manager of a local cooperative that owned several businesses, including the *Southern Consumers Times*. It was a Friday evening routine for our group of five Black men to sit in Mac's office, eating boudin and sipping wine, while wrangling about local, state, and national politics. The walls of Mac's office, lined with African artifacts and framed prints of Nelson Mandela, Malcolm X, and Reverend Martin Luther King Jr., provided the perfect backdrop. For me, one of only a handful of Black people who worked at city hall, it was an opportunity to connect with friends whom I had once worked with and to have my finger on the pulse of current social and political developments of the local Black community.

That day, Je'Nelle Chargois, the manager of *Southern Consumers Times*, showed up with a cassette tape player. She had been working on a project for a special Lafayette centennial edition of the paper, in which she orally captured the stories of old Black residents of the city. We listened to a few of the recordings.

In one recording, Mr. Jeanlouis, a man in his mideighties, told the story of Emile Hebert's trial. I vaguely remembered hearing my mother tell parts of the story years before about an older brother of my grandfather. "I think that's my great-uncle," I said excitedly, after hearing the story. And so, my research began.

I visited Mr. Jeanlouis and gathered more facts. He had known Emile Hebert and gone to the trial. He even remembered the names of Hebert's attorneys. I delved into newspaper articles and court records and eventually wrote a story of Hebert's trial for the newspaper's centennial issue.

Twenty-five years later, as a creative writing graduate student at the University of New Orleans, I began to look deeper into details of Emile

81

Hebert's case. It was then that I discovered the Mer Rouge murders and Governor Parker's relentless efforts to stop the growing influence of the Ku Klux Klan in Louisiana. Only then did I fully appreciate the historical significance of Emile Hebert's case.

A narrative of the trial was written in several genres before this novella. In 2009, I wrote a two-act play of the trial while at the University of New Orleans. Several people were especially supportive in my writing the play. Phil Lank, a former supervisor in Lafayette city government and a close friend for many years, provided constant encouragement. He led me to Dr. David Cheramie, former Executive Director of CODOFIL, Council for the Development of French in Louisiana, who provided Cajun-Creole French translations that appear in the play and in this book. Jules Edwards, a former judge of the 15th Judicial District Court in Lafayette, read the play and shared knowledge on Louisiana law and criminal trial court proceedings. In 2014, I wrote a poem titled "Soul Be A Witness," that captured the testimony of ten people speaking in the Hebert trial, including the judge, prosecutor, defense attorneys, witnesses, and jury foreman. The poem appeared in my collection titled *Soul Be A Witness*. I am deeply indebted to MadHat Press for publishing the book.

Thank you to the Hebert family, especially Ron Hebert and Michael Hebert, grandsons of Emile, for believing that this book would be published and for their many expressions of gratitude that I was persevering. My cousins Stacey L. Zeno, the keeper of our family's ancestry, and Stephanie Jones, a granddaughter of John Hebert, were also very supportive in providing facts on Hebert family history.

I wrote this book during the COVID-19 pandemic. Disheartened that I could not do public readings in my service as Poet Laureate of Louisiana and hunkered down on my patio for sixteen hours a day, I decided to follow the suggestion of Devon E. Lord, editor-in-chief of UL Press, and expanded the play that I had written as a graduate student into a novella. I am deeply grateful to her for the advice she gave me in structuring the story and editing the narrative. Special thanks to Dr. Michael S. Martin, history professor at the University of Louisiana at Lafayette, for his close reading of the manuscript and for the corrections he offered to ensure historical accuracy of the text.

Last, my thanks to Robert Mann, Dr. Rick Swanson, and Dr. Lawrence Powell for reading the manuscript and providing comments that appear on the back cover.

News Articles

Monument To General Alfred Mouton, Which Is To Be Unveiled Saturday Afternoon

MONUMENT AND GROUNDS FORM BEAUTY SCENE

Statue of Italian Marble And Other Features Make Most Pleasing Sight.

Standing at the intersection of Lee and Jefferson Avenues, at a point centrally located, the Mouton Monument presents an imposing sight, made all the more so by the fine arrangement of grounds surrounding the monument.

The site was donated for the purpose by the city, which had in turn secured it from the estate of Archille Fingaro, who incidently was for many years employed by Governor and United States Senator Alexanler Mouton, father of General Alfred Mouton. In view of this fact, special concessions were secured by the city in securing the property.

A building which was originally on the site was moved, and a short street running from Jefferson to Lee at one side of the grounds was closed, affording more space.

Contract for the monument was let in June, 1921 to F. R. Blakesley, contractor of this city, Franklin, Crowley and New Iberia and for many years engaged in monument work.

From a photograph of General Mouton a sketch was prepared, with scale to assure proper size of the monument, and this sketch was forwarded to Cararra, Italy.

The statue was made in Italy and is of Ruthland Italian marble. Some time was required for its making and shipment to this city, but in the meantime work was pushed on the base of the monument and on the grounds surrounding.

The monument from street level measures 21 feet in heighth. The base is of Pitsford Valley Marble, as well as the several posts surrounding the grounds, and which are connected by a series of chains. On the four sides of the base are inscriptions pertaining to principal facts connected with General Mouton's life.

On the grounds at three sides of the monument are large cement vases. In addition there is also a five point star of cement in the center of which is a smaller vase. A system of cement walks is provided and there is also cement curbing surrounding the grounds. A small stone, with the name of the contractor thereon, occupies a point to one side of the monument.

During the construction of the monument and grounds work was under way both during the daytime and at night for a certain period, lights having been provided so that nights could be utilized in an effort to complete the work more rapidly.

The first intention was to have the unveiling in February, but decision was reached to advance the date until April 8th, making the anniversary of the date on which General Mouton lost his life in the Battle of Mansfield, 1864.

—Curb Market Saturday—

Daily Advertiser, April 7, 1922

AUSTIN LANDRY OF RAYNE KILLED.
SHERIFF LATIOLAIS AND JULES BROUSSARD WOUNDED BY NEGRO

Emile Hebert, Brother And Wife Arrested As Result Of Shooting Near Youngsville Tuesday Night—Arrests Made This Morning Following Some Hard Work On Part Of Local Officers And Others—Black Removed This Morning For Safe-Keeping—Hebert And Wife Were In Buggy—Sheriff And Other Men Were Returning From Abbeville And Had Gone To Get Assistance In Getting Car Out Of Mud.

Austin P. Landry, of Rayne, was killed and Sheriff Felix Latiolais of this city and Jules Broussard, of near Youngsville, were wounded Tuesday night, as the result of a shooting tragedy near the refinery at Youngsville.

Emile Hebert, a negro, and also his wife and a brother were being held today. According to announcement made this morning by officers, Emile Hebert confessed to the shooting and told practically the same story of the shooting as did his wife.

Information from the Sheriff's office this morning was to the effect that the shooting took place about 11:00 o'clock Tuesday night on the road near the Youngsville refinery. Sheriff Latiolais, together with Austin Landry and Julius Delahoussaye, one of the jockeys at the Fair Grounds track here, were returning from Abbeville, when their car became stuck in a muddy section of road.

They went to the refinery to secure assistance in getting the car out, it is stated, and were joined by Jules Broussard and a younger brother, the men then starting back toward the car. On their way they met Emile Hebert and his wife, who together with their three months old baby were returning from the home of Hebert's father, where they are said to have spent the evening.

The negro is said to have demanded that the men walking in the road give him the right of way and it is stated that they complied by moving to one side. Some words are then understood to have followed, and the negro is said to have used some strong language.

Hebert, it is stated, then pulled a single barrel shotgun from the buggy and fired, Landry being struck below the heart.

Sheriff Latiolais was carrying a spade which had been secured for use in getting the automobile out of the mud, and as the negro shot, the officer struck at the buggy with the spade, it is stated, also pulling out his revolver at the same time.

The force of the blow from the spade is said to have knocked Hebert's wife from the buggy into the road, the vehicle passing over her, and also the three months' old baby which she was carrying in her arms. The woman appeared to be uninjured this morning however, except for a bruise on the head. The baby escaped injury.

Daily Advertiser, June 21, 1922

As the negro fired a second time, Sheriff Latiolais also fired, it is stated, but missed. The negro's second shot tore through the Sheriff's side and struck Broussard in the forehead and breast. Young Delahoussaye, who had been near the automobile during the shooting was not struck, and the younger Broussard also escaped injury.

The injured men were taken to the office of Drs. Comeaux and Dupuis, at Youngsville, where they were attended by Drs. R. K. and A. J. Comeaux, and Dr. J. W. Dupuis, and afterwards removed to the home of Dr. R. K. Comeaux where Landry died an hour later. Sheriff Latiolais was removed to his home this morning.

Following the shooting officers here were notified and went to the scene. Deputy Sheriffs R. H. Broussard and George Breaux, together with Mayor Parent and City Marshal Stutes, of Youngsville, went to the home of John Hebert, a brother of Emile Hebert and arrested the former, taking him back to Youngsville where he was placed in charge of Mayor Parent and Marshal Stutes.

From Youngsville a visit was then made to the home of Henry Hebert, father of Emile Hebert, about a mile north of Youngsville and gathered information that the son had spent part of the evening there.

Occupants of htree cars from here joined in the search for the negro. In one car was City Marshal Cas Chargois, Police Officer Frank Gulley, Warren Lacoste and J. B. Mouton, while Deputy Sheriff R. H. Broussard, Police Officer Albert Daspit, C. D. Pitre and A. Garret were in another car, and Deputy

Sheriffs Milton Campbell and Geo. Breaux and Aldus Alleman and City Marshal Stutes of Youngsville were in the other car.

When the members of the party arrived at the home of Herbert near Vermillion parish about 5 o'clock this morning, it is stated that the negro was coming from a barn near the house and that his wife was in the house asleep.

Herbert did not resist arrest. He was brought back to this city in one car and his wife in the other. It is said that the clothes worn by the couple Suesday night had been washed and apparently other steps taken to remove any signs of the tragedy.

Information obtained by the officers from Charley Harrison, a negro residing near Youngsville was to the effect that Hebert and his wife went to Harrison's home following the shooting and that they told of the trouble. Harrison told the officers that he had found the gun, which had evidently been abandoned by Hebert. The latter declared that he had thrown the gun in a field.

On the way back to this city the members of the party bringing Hebert met the negro's father and asked him if the son had been at his house Tuesday night. The father is said to have admitted that this was so.

Hebert was placed in the parish jail and his wife in the city jail For safe-keeping Hebert was later removed this morning to Franklin, in custody of Parish Jailer Sim J. Boudreaux and Deputy Sheriff's George Breaux and Milton Campbell.

Due to the weakened condition of Sheriff Latiolais this morning it was not deemed advisable to permit an interview with him in regard to details of the shooting. Although the wound, which is on the left-hand side of the body, below the heart, is considered dangerous, it is believed that he has a good chance for recovery.

HEBERT MURDER TRIAL IS SET FOR MONDAY

IS CHARGED WITH MURDER IN CONNECTION WITH SHOOTING ON JUNE 20TH

The trial of Emile Hebert, negro, indicted by the recent grand jury on a charge of murder, is set to open Monday in District Court here.

Attorneys John L. Kennedy and Sidney Roos are to handle the defense in the trial, while the prosecution will be in charge of District Attorney Percy Ogden.

Hebert was indicted on a charge growing out of the shooting near Youngsville on the night of June 20th, which resulted in the death of Austin P. Landry, of Rayne, and the wounding of Sheriff Felix Latiolais of this city, and Jules Broussard, residing near Youngsville.

A number of witnesses have been summoned in connection with the trial, it was stated this morning at the Clerk of Court's office.

Several other cases are also scheduled for hearing in District Court next week on different charges.

Daily Advertiser, October 21, 1922

TROOPS TO GUARD NEGRO HERE NEXT WEEK, INDICATED

Information Today Hints That National Guards Will Be Used During Trial

Information at the Sheriff's office this morning indicated strongly that National Guardsmen will be placed on duty here next week to protect Emile Hebert, negro, during his trial on a murder charge.

A copy of a letter from Adjutant General Tombs to Major E. P. Roy, of the Second Battalion, La. National Guards, received at the Sheriff's office referred to a request received from Judge Wm. Campbell for troops to safe-guard Hebert during the trial which is scheduled to open Monday in District Court, and ordered Major Roy to prepare to proceed to this city to assume charge.

Indication was made in the letter that members of the National Guard company here would be available for duty.

Information secured here this morning, however, was to the effect that no definite orders had been received in regard to use of the local Guardsmen. It is thought probable that some of the men from other nearby companies may also be included in the orders.

Daily Advertiser, October 21, 1922

TROOPS ON DUTY HERE AS TRIAL OF NEGRO STARTS

New Iberia Guardsmen Arrived This Morning And Established Camp

SEARCH IS MADE

Those Going Into Court Room Today Were Examined for Weapons

Court House Square presented a military appearance this morning as National Guardsmen of Company E, 156 Infantry, at New Iberia, went on duty during the trial of Emile Hebert, negro, charged with murder in connection with the shooting near Youngsville last June, and which resulted in the death of Austin P. Landry, and injuries to Sheriff Felix Latiolais and Jules Broussard.

The Guardsmen numbering 48, arrived from New Iberia early this morning, in charge of Captain Warren Jefferson. Major E. P. Roy, of the Second Battalion, La. National Guards, whose home is also at New Iberia, is in general charge.

The troops were sent in as a precautionary measure, reports having been current that an attempt would be made to secure Hebert. Orders were dispatched to Major Roy at New Iberia, by Adjutant Tombs, following a request from Judge William Campbell.

Tents were being pitched and a camp established by the troops this morning. The Guardsmen were stationed on the Court House grounds, and also placed on duty in the court room and other positions in the court house. Persons entering the court room were searched for any weapons, as a further measure of caution.

The larger part of today was expected to be occupied in securing a jury for the trial. Up to noon three members of the jury had been secured, it was announced. District Attorney Percy Ogden is in charge of the prosecution while the defense is represented by John L. Kennedy and Sidney Roos.

Today was the first time in the history of the parish, it was stated, that troops have been used in connection with a trial here.

The trial is expected to occupy several days. At the opening of this morning's session the court room was about half-filled, the rain evidently cutting down the attendance.

Daily Advertiser, October 23, 1922

COMPLETE JURY IN HEBERT TRIAL

The work of securing the jury in the trial of Emile Hebert negro charged with murder, was completed shortly before noon today, and adjournment was then taken until 1:30 this afternoon at which time the hearing of the trial was scheduled to start.

Four members of the jury were secured Monday, before the exhaustion of the regular venire of thirty names, and adjournment was then taken until this morning for the purpose of issuing summons to fifty whose names were on the detalybus jury list.

The four jurymen secured Monday were Luc Langlinais, Linex Hoffpauir, Eraste C. Landry and Chas. McDonald and the other members of the jury, secured this morning, are Lot Tarver, Ivy Tarver, Alex D. Verot, L. P. DeBlanc, Fred Voorhies, F. J. Voorhies, Walter B. Block, and Leonard L. Bourgeois.

Members of Company E, New Iberia National Guards, remain on duty on the court house grounds and in the court room, and are to be stationed here throughout the trial as a matter of precaution against any move to secure Hebert, following rumors that this would be attempted.

Besides the New Iberia troops, some of the members of Machine Company M, National Guard, of this city, have also been ordered out, for night duty. A detachment of twelve men from the local company, went on guard Monday night, in command of First Lieutenant Alfred Moss.

Daily Advertiser, October 24, 1922

MURDER TRIAL ENTERS SECOND DAY

INDICATED THIS MORNING THAT NIGHT SESSION OF TRIAL MIGHT BE HELD

The trial of Emile Hebert, negro, charged with murder, entered the second day this morning, with indications that the trial will not be completed until late today or possibly Thursday.

It was thought possible that a night session might be held tonight if there is an opportunity to complete the trial at that time. Indications were today, however, that the hearing would continue the larger part of Thursday.

Several witnesses were placed on the stand Tuesday afternoon and also this morning, by the State, with the defense witnesses to appear later. Sheriff Felix Latiolais, who was injured in the shooting in connection with which Hebert is being tried, was the principal witness at Tuesday afternoon's session. It was reported today that the condition of Jules Broussard, who was also injured in the shooting, is such that he will be unable to appear as a witness.

Quarters have been arranged in the court room for the use of the members of the jury at night during the trial.

There was a large crowd on hand for the session of the trial Tuesday afternoon, and also this morning.

Daily Advertiser, October 25, 1922

MURDER CASE RESULTS IN MISTRIAL

ANNOUNCEMENT MADE THAT MORNING THAT JURY COULD NOT APGFE IN FMILE HEBERT CASE

The trial of Emile Hebert, negro, charged with murder in connection with the shooting near Youngsville last June, resulting in the death of Austin P. Landry, of Rayne, and injuries to Sheriff Felix Latiolais of this city and Jules Broussard, of near Youngsville, ended this morning in a mis-trial, the jury being unable to agree upon a verdict, it was announced by the foreman, L. P. De Blanc.

Arguments in the trial closed shortly after 6 o'clock Wednesday evening, and the case was given to the jury. At 7 o'clock, Judge Campbell was advised that no agreement had been reached and adjourned court, the jury being retained in the quarters arranged for them in the court house.

At 9 o'clock this morning, following the opening of court, the jury was called, and the foreman reported that the jury has been unable to agree Judge Campbell then discharged the eight jurymen who had been taken from the detalybus jury list, the four who had been taken from the regular jury panel being retained for further service.

Shortly after the close of the trial, the New Iberia National Guardsmen who have been on duty at the court house since the opening of the hearing, left for their homes by train.

Hebert was removed today from the Parish Jail here to another city.

The trial which was a hard fought one has attracted considerable interest, and large crowds have been in attendance. Attorneys John L. Kennedy and Sidney Roos were counsel for the defense, and District Attorney Percy Ogden conducted the prosecution.

Daily Advertiser, October 26, 1922

KLANSMEN RENEW MER ROUGE TERROR

Residents Appeal Against Reprisals Following the Start of a Federal Inquiry.

Special to The New York Times.

BATON ROUGE, La., Nov. 26.—An appeal to Governor John M. Parker and the Federal authorities for protection against a threatened invasion by the Ku Klux Klan of the little town of Mer Rouge, in Morehouse Parish, in retaliation for information given to Department of Justice investigators relative to the disappearance of five persons and the reported murder of two is contained in a statement signed by a committee of Mer Rouge residents.

Department of Justice agents have been in Morehouse Parish for weeks. They have been there openly and in some cases under cover. The Post Office Department has conducted an investigation also.

One witness, who told the Federal agents that he was forced to carry water for a hooded mob, and who is reported to have seen several of the mob with their masks off, was taken from his home and is being hidden for safekeeping. Federal operatives are conducting the investigation of the kidnapping because of the belief that members of the mob come from across the Arkansas line, with leaders even from more distant states.

It is known that the Federal agents have what they believe is positive information that the bodies of the two missing men are in Lake La Fourche, near Oak Ridge, and that the bodies were dropped into the lake bound to two large iron wheels picked up from the shore.

The statement of the citizens declares that the article in a Washington newspaper relative to conditions in Louisiana is true as far as Morehouse Parish is concerned. It reads in part:

" We do not know conditions all over the State, but we, as citizens of Mer Rouge, know that our parish, Morehouse Parish, is being dominated by the Invisible Empire. Several of our citizens have been threatened. The safety of every one has been threatened if they even voice criticism of the Klan for kidnapping five of our citizens, beating and whipping two of them and making off with two others, whom we believe now to have been foully murdered.

" The Klan dominates Morehouse Parish. The administrative machinery of the local Government is so broken down that it is practically impossible either to indict or convict members of the Klan for their violations of the law.

" For weeks Mer Rouge has been prepared, rifles and revolvers at hand, for the threatened invasion of our village by the Klan force. Telephones have been cut and we feared invasion. We appeal for protection, appeal to the State and to the Federal Government. This is in no sense a reflection on Governor Parker, from whom we expect and believe we will get aid and protection.

" Now that The Washington Post and Mr. Browne are under fire, we invite Mr. Browne to come to Morehouse Parish and take evidence to show not only that all he said in his first article in reference to conditions in Louisiana is true as far as Morehouse Parish is concerned, but also to show that conditions are even worse."

The statement is signed by W. B. Stuckey, attorney; W. F. Campbell, the Town Marshal; A. C. Whipple, a garage proprietor, and C. A. Brunson.

An attack on one of the Department of Justice agents was planned, according to these citizens, but the agent, ignorant of the plans, left town in the afternoon of the day the raid was to be made. This circumstance, they declare, is all that prevented a battle between the opposing forces.

New York Times, November 27, 1922

SHADOW OF KU KLUX KLAN GROWS LARGER IN CONGRESS AND NATION

Seventy-Five Members of the House Reported Elected by Its Votes—Well-Known Legislators Defeated—Growth in Indiana and Other Northern States Deemed Significant.

THE seriousness of the Ku Klux menace in certain parts of the United States was brought home when it became known that John M. Parker, Governor of Louisiana, had gone to Washington seeking the help of the National Government in combating the "invisible empire."

It is common talk in Washington that the next Congress will have many men who are members of, or in sympathy with, the Ku Klux Klan. According to one report, probably seventy-five men in the new Congress will owe their election in large part to the support of the masked organization. It is established that there will be Representatives in the Congress who come to Washington with Klan endorsement. Whether they are members is a question which cannot be answered, for the Klansman, as a rule, does not admit his membership. He either denies it in a guarded sort of fashion or refuses to answer the question.

That the Ku Klux problem has assumed nation-wide proportions cannot longer be denied. Senator Walsh of Massachusetts, Chairman of the National Democratic Senatorial Committee, charged on the floor of the Senate that "the Klan showed its heinous and venomous character here and there in the recent election," and that, encouraged by its own power in some States, the organization "is threatening control of the political machinery of our political parties."

The words of Senator Walsh were startling, but what he said has been borne out by reports from all parts of the country, particularly the South and West, where the growth of the Klan has been greatest. In at least two States—Texas and Oregon—it has proved its strength; in one case by the election of a Senator alleged to have been a member of the Klan and in the other by the election of a Governor. Instance after instance in which members of Congress, State officials and lesser officials have been defeated because of Klan opposition are cited in political circles.

Because of the position Governor Parker has assumed, the situation in Louisiana is the most talked about of all the States in the Union, but conditions in Louisiana are no worse than in a number of other States. In Louisiana the Klan is charged with the kidnapping and murder of several citizens; it is alleged that it has elected the Mayor of one of Louisiana's largest cities (not New Orleans), and that in some sections in the northern part of the State it has assumed a dominating position.

In Indiana, if Washington reports are true, and the evidence is that they have not been exaggerated, the Klan has made more headway, from a political point of view, than in any other State in the Central West. The Klan in Indiana exerted its influence in a large number of instances in the recent election. The defeat of Milton Kraus, a veteran member of Congress, was attributed to the activities of the masked organization. Another reported victim of the organization was William J. Oliver, Republican candidate for State Treasurer. A third was Patrick J. Lynch, who stood for re-election as Clerk of the Indiana Supreme Court.

Religious Issue Dominates.

The only known ground for the opposition of the Klan to these men was that of religion. Kraus is a Jew, Lynch a Catholic, and Oliver was said to have married a member of that Church. Had the rest of the Republican State ticket gone down to defeat, the charge that the Ku Klux had contributed to the defeat of Oliver and Lynch would have collapsed, but the remainder of the Republican State ticket, in all important instances, was elected.

The defeat of Kraus was one of the surprises. For six years he had been a member of the lower House and by common consent one of its hardest working and most conscientious members. He was a native of Indiana and had lived most of his life in the little city of Peru, a prominent lawyer. He was defeated by Samuel E. Cook of Huntington. Mr. Cook was said not to be a member of the Klan and made no plea for the support of the "invisible empire." But, as in the case of Brewster in Missouri, who was against the Klan, he got its support, mainly because Kraus belonged to a race proscribed by the Klan.

Another Indiana candidate alleged to have been a victim of the Klan was L. J. Quill of Indianapolis, the Republican candidate for Clerk of Marion County. And there were others, so the story goes, in Washington. The greatest strength of the Indiana organization is in the cities. Indianapolis, Terre Haute, Fort Wayne and Logansport. The negro population of Indianapolis is proportionately one of the largest of any city in the North.

In the neighboring State of Ohio the Ku Klux is also at work, if information in Washington is correct. Two Democratic candidates there for the House of Representatives, whose election was practically conceded, were said to have gone down to defeat because of Klan opposition. These candidates were J. H. Goeke, defeated by John L. Cable in the Fourth District, and William A. Ashbrook, overwhelmed by William M. Morgan in the Seventeenth District. Ashbrook was one of the most prominent Democrats in the State and a two-to-one favorite. Although neither Cable nor Morgan was of the Klan, they nevertheless were said to have received the practically solid support of the Ku Klux units in the Fourth and Seventeenth Districts.

Out in Missouri it was the Ku Klux Klan and not the Woodrow Wilson influence which threatened to defeat Senator Reed. Two weeks before the election St. Louis was conceded to Reed by from 40,000 to 50,000 and Kansas City by from 15,000 to 25,000. Mr. Reed's opponent, Reginald R. Brewster, like Reed, was an uncompromising foe of the Klan, but Reed decided that Senator Reed was the more dangerous of the two and threw its support to his Republican opponent. A few days before the election the organization held a great meeting in Kansas City, with an estimated attendance of something like 15,000 persons. Then, on election day, the Klan showed its strength, and Reed lost Kansas City by about 400 votes, instead of carrying it by 15,000 or more. The Klan vote in the city has been estimated at about 12,000, which was the vote received by one of its admitted candidates. In other

Continued from previous page

strong Klan centres in Missouri the vote was correspondingly impressive.

Across the line from Missouri is Kansas, another State where, if reports are true, the "invisible empire" has been making great headway. Representative Philip Campbell, Chairman of the House Committee on Rules, was head of the House Committee which investigated the Ku Klux Klan last year. He was badly defeated when he stood for renomination, and will not be in the next Congress. So serious has the Kansas situation become that Governor Allen is said to be planning a State-wide investigation of the organization in the hope of "unmasking" it and bringing such members as have violated the law to justice.

Won for Arkansas Governor.

To the south of Kansas are Arkansas and Oklahoma, and in both of those States the Ku Klux is admittedly gaining strength every day and it has become a commanding influence in the political affairs of large sections of both Commonwealths. In Arkansas at the recent election every candidate for office in Pulaski County, the seat of which is Little Rock, the State capital, who had the endorsement of the Klan was elected. Every man who stood for office on an anti-Klan ticket was beaten. Governor McRae, said to have had the Klan endorsement, swept the primaries with a two to one majority over his opponent, Judge Toney. In the Fifth Congressional District Heartsill Ragon, elected to succeed H. M. Jacoway, had the Klan endorsement. In the primary he won the nomination over a field of four strong opponents. Returns in other parts of the State were just as interesting from a Ku Klux point of view. The same story of the continued extension of its sphere of influence comes from Oklahoma.

Next in line is Texas, which shares with Oregon the distinction of being the banner Ku Klux State of the Union. In Texas, as everybody knows, the Klan had grown so powerful that it was able to nominate and subsequently elect the candidate it had endorsed for the United States Senate. This Senator-elect is Earle B. Mayfield of Austin, whose right to the seat is now the subject of bitter controversy in that State, and which may be challenged when Mr. Mayfield presents his credentials at the bar of the Senate next March.

It would be hard to exaggerate the Texas situation, if the stories told in Washington are true. So bitter has the fight become that it has estranged lifelong friends, and in some instances, so it is alleged, even destroyed the relations of Texas families. An illustration of the Klan dominance in parts of the State was the defeat of "Bob" Buchanan, the famous border Sheriff, who has fought the Klan "morning, noon and night," in his own words, and went to defeat because of his courage.

The upset of Harry Hertzberg of San Antonio, the Democratic nominee for Congress from the Fourteenth, or San Antonio, District was charged principally to the Ku Klux Klan. Hertzberg, a Jew of the highest standing, was opposed by Harry Wurzbach, a Republican, who defeated him in this normally heavy Democratic district by 4,000 votes.

The writer asked a Texan now in Washington in a high official capacity about the situation in the Lone Star State.

"There can, be," he said, "no two opinions as to the Ku Klux situation in Texas. The organization is out to control the State, and it has made great headway. It has elected a Senator, in some instances the Judges who will preside over our courts, and probably has a majority in the lower house of the Texas Legislature. The number of officers, such as Sheriffs and other local and county officials, who owe their election to the Ku Klux it is impossible to estimate.

"Dallas County is, in point of population, the principal county of Texas, and in that county the Klan made a clean sweep, among the officials it carried into office being three Judges. On election night the Klan openly celebrated its victory. A horde of the Klansmen paraded through the streets of Dallas, and when they passed the headquarters of Mr. Peddie, the independent candidate who sought to defeat Mayfield, tore down every flag and other sign or insignia in front of his headquarters. They are great winners and mighty poor losers. As in Dallas, they celebrated in their own fashion the victory of Mayfield in other cities and towns of the State. Mayfield says that he has resigned from the Klan. Whether that be so or not is of little consequence. The big fact is that he was elected by Klan votes, and for that reason there are thousands of good Texans who are going to do their level best to keep him out of the Senate."

Oregon is face to face with a Ku Klux menace of the first magnitude. Governor B. W. Olcott, an implacable foe of the organization, and backed by the anti-Klan forces regardless of party, was swept out of office on Nov. 7 by a majority of more than 33,000 votes. His opponent had the Klan endorsement. The Klan also put over its school program, which makes it compulsory for children between the ages of 8 and 16 years to attend the public schools. This proposed law is aimed principally at the Roman Catholic Church and would, it is said, outlaw practically every parochial school in the State.

For years the most popular member of the Oregon delegation in the lower house of Congress has been Clifton N. McArthur of Portland. McArthur opposed the bonus and woman suffrage and both contributed to his defeat. But the Klan influence was the strongest element.

A Southern State where the Klan seems to have been checkmated is Mississippi. In the Vardaman-Stephens primary fight for the Senatorial nomination every effort was made to line up the Klan hordes on the side of ex-Senator Vardaman, it was said. But Stephens won and will be the successor of John Sharp Williams in the next Senate. In the Eighth Mississippi Congressional District the Klan sought the defeat of James W. Collier of Vicksburg, for fourteen years a member of the lower house. He won the nomination by a largely reduced majority.

Other States whence come reports of Klan activities include Illinois, Kentucky, Tennessee, California, Arizona, Connecticut, Massachusetts, Maryland, Virginia, North Dakota and even New York. But in these States it has not been able so far to make the showing it has elsewhere. That it is spreading and seeks to operate nationally no one denies. To further its political program it has started to recruit an auxiliary of women.

The Government in Washington realizes the seriousness of the situation. That the war on the masked horde is about to begin in earnest is the opinion of informed people in the capital.

LAFAYETTE KLAN MEMBERS RESIGN

Organization Surrenders Charter As Means of Restoring Harmony to Community.

Lafayette, La., April 5.—Denying that their motive was one of religious intolerance or anti-Catholic or anti-Jewish in spirit, but saying that they realize it is the popular belief of the Catholics and Jews of the community that the Ku Klux Klan is anti-Catholic and anti-Jewish in spirit and purpose, members of the Lafayette Klan, B. C. Crow 24, have voted to resign from the order, disband and return the charter of the leading officials of the "Invisible Empire."

The action was taken at a special meeting of the local klan as a result of unrest caused during the last few days by the distribution of a printed list purporting to contain the names of all members of the Lafayette klan. A resolution to disband was adopted and was made public accompanied by sworn statements from J. B. Vanness, secretary or kliagraff, pertaining to the minutes of the meeting and the resolution, and from Charles M. Parkerson, L. O. Clark and S. R. Parkerson as follows:

"A special meeting of the Lafayette Klan, B. C. Crow 24, met in session today to consider the question hereinafter acted upon. The following resolution was offered and being duly seconded was adopted:

"'Resolved that whereas, the members of the Lafayette Klan, B. C. Crow 24, joined and organized a klan in this community from motives, which, it is useless to say, and still less useles to argue, were honorable, and which would redound to the welfare of our country; and,

"'Whereas, our motive was not one of religious intolerance or anti-Catholic or anti-Jewish spirit, as exemplified by our past conduct in our active and substantial assistance in a pecuniary way, when the occasion arose in Catholic activities, in our personal relations with the Catholic clergy and our fellow citizens of these persuasions, and in some instances in our domestic relations, including our active consent to the membership of our own children in the Catholic Church; and,

"'Whereas, we now realize that it is the popular belief of the Catholics and the Jews of this community that the Ku Klux Klan is anti-Catholic and anti-Jewish in spirit and purpose, and is calculated to disrupt the spirit of harmony and religious tolerance which is so well established in our constitutions, state and federal, and which is so essential to the tranquility and prosperity of our city; now therefore, it is

"'Resolved, That the members of the Lafayette Klan, B. C. Crow 24, now disband resign as members of the organization and return their charter.'

"The meeting then adjourned.
"April 4, 1923.
    (Seal)   "J. B. VANNESS,
                    "Kliagraff.
"Lafayette, La., April 4, 1923.

"I hereby certify that the above and foregoing is a true and correct copy of the minutes of the proceedings of Lafayette Klan, B. C. Crow No. 24, and a true and correct copy of the resolution adopted by said organization at a special meeting held on April 3, 1923. In witness whereof, I have affixed my signature and the seal of the Lafayette Klan, B. C. Crow No. 24, at Lafayette, La., this 4th day of April, A. D., 1923.
    (Signed)   "J. B. VANNESS,
                    "Kliagraff."

"The above resolution and certification were sworn before Orther C. Mouton of Mouton & Debaillon, notary public, April 4, 1923. Sworn statement was also sworn before notary.
    (Signed)
    "CHARLES M. PARKERSON,
    "L. O. CLARK,
    "S. R. PARKERSON."

Don't bite the hand that's feeding you.

Crowley Signal, April 7, 1923

BIBLIOGRAPHY

"Austin Landry of Rayne Killed, Sheriff Latiolais and Jules Broussard Wounded by Negro." *Daily Advertiser* (Lafayette, LA), June 21, 1922.

Battle of Liberty Place Monument. The Historical Marker Database. Retrieved October 28, 2010. https://www.hmdb.org/m. asp?m=34742.

Blokker, Laura Ewen. "The African American Experience in Louisiana." State of Louisiana Department of Culture, Recreation, and Tourism, May 15, 2012. https://www.crt.state.la.us/Assets/OCD/ hp/nationalregister/historic_contexts/The_African_American_ Experience_in_Louisiana.pdf.

Boissoneault, Lorraine. "The Deadliest Massacre in Reconstruction-Era Louisiana Happened 150 Years Ago." *Smithsonian Magazine*, September 28, 2018. https://www.smithsonianmag.com/history/ story-deadliest-massacre-reconstruction-era-louisiana-180970420/.

"Broussard, Edwin Sidney." Biographical Directory of the United States Congress. Retrieved July 1, 2021. https://bioguide.congress.gov/ search/bio/B000895.

Brown, Yvonne. "Tolerance and Bigotry in Southwest Louisiana: The Ku Klux Klan, 1921–23." *Louisiana History* 47, no. 2 (2006): 153–68.

"Complete Jury in Hebert Trial." *Daily Advertiser* (Lafayette, LA), October 24, 1922.

DeSantis, John. *The Thibodaux Massacre: Racial Violence and the 1887 Sugarcane Labor Strike.* Charleston, SC: The History Press, 2016.

Dier, Chris. "October 25, 1968: St. Bernard Parish Massacre." Zinn Education Project. Retrieved July 12, 2021. https://www. zinnedproject.org/news/tdih/st-bernard-parish-massacre.

"Emile Hebert: A Place in Lafayette's History." *Southern Consumers Times* (Lafayette, LA), May 1984.

Fairclough, Adam. *Race & Democracy: The Civil Rights Struggle in Louisiana, 1915–1972*. Athens: University of Georgia Press, 1995.

"The FBI Versus the Klan." Los Angeles Community Policing, February 26, 2010. Retrieved May 24, 2012. http://www.lacp.org/2010-Articles-Main/103010-FBIvsKlan-3parts.htm.

Federal Bureau of Investigation. Memo of September 25, 1922. FBI Archives. Retrieved June 2, 2008. https://archives.fbi.gov/archives/news/stories/2010/april/klan2_042910/memo-of-september-25-1922.

"Felix Mariam Latiolais Sr." Find A Grave. Retrieved October 5, 2010. https://www.findagrave.com/memorial/173027143/felix-mariam-latiolais.

"Filmore Watt Daniel." Find A Grave. Retrieved June 26, 2020. https://www.findagrave.com/memorial/44235131/filmore-watt-daniel.

Fortier, Alcee, ed. "Percy T. Ogden." In *Louisiana: Comprising Sketches of Parishes, Towns, Events, Institutions, and Persons, Arranged in Cyclopedic Form*, vol. 3, 336–39. Madison, WI: Century Historical Association, 1914. Retrieved from US GenWeb Archives, October 5, 2010. http://files.usgwarchives.net/la/acadia/bios/biosk-p/ogden.txt.

Gagliano, Katie. "Confederate Mouton statue removed from downtown Lafayette: 'It represents freedom.'" *Acadiana Advocate* (Lafayette, LA), July 17, 2021. https://www.theadvocate.com/acadiana/news/article_38495e88-e73b-11eb-a747-e786eaeb9c73.html

Gates, Henry Louis, Jr., and Valerie A. Smith. *The Norton Anthology of African American Literature*. 3rd ed. New York: W. W. Norton & Company, 2014.

Gordon, Linda. *The Second Coming of the KKK: The Ku Klux Klan of the 1920s and the American Political Tradition*. New York: Liveright Publishing Corporation, 2017.

Harrell, Kenneth Earl. "The Ku Klux Klan in Louisiana, 1920–1930." PhD diss., Louisiana State University, 1966.

"Hebert Murder Trial Is Set for Monday." *Daily Advertiser* (Lafayette, LA), October 21, 1922.

"History of Franklin." Cajun Coast Visitors and Convention Bureau. Retrieved May 30, 2022. https://www.cajuncoast.com/about-us/history/history-franklin.

"Hylan Praises Parker for Fight on Klan." *New York Times,* December 24, 1922.

Ingram, Alton Earl. "The Twentieth Century Ku Klux Klan in Morehouse Parish, Louisiana." PhD diss., Louisiana State University, 1961.

"John L. Kennedy, Lafayette Atty. Dies at Biloxi." *Abbeville Progress* (Abbeville, LA), September 7, 1929.

"John Parker." 64 Parishes. Retrieved July 1, 2021. https://64parishes. org/entry/john-parker.

"Judge William Campbell." Find A Grave. Retrieved July 2, 2020. https://www.findagrave.com/memorial/155095146/ william-campbell.

"Klansmen Renew Mer Rouge Terror." *New York Times,* November 27, 1922.

"Lafayette Klan Members Resign: Organization Surrenders Charter as Means of Restoring Harmony to Community." *Crowley Signal* (Crowley, LA), April 7, 1923.

Lewis, Danny. "The 1873 Colfax Massacre Crippled the Reconstruction Era." *Smithsonian Magazine,* April 13, 2016. https://www. smithsonianmag.com/smart-news/1873-colfax-massacre-crippled- reconstruction-180958746/.

"Monument and Grounds Form Beauty Scene." *Daily Advertiser* (Lafayette, LA), April 7, 1922.

"Mouton Monument Is Unveiled with Impressive Program, and Is Witnessed By Large Crowd." *Daily Advertiser,* (Lafayette, LA), April 10, 1922.

"Murder Case Results in Mistrial." *Daily Advertiser* (Lafayette, LA), October 26, 1922.

"Murder Trial Enters Second Day." *Daily Advertiser* (Lafayette, LA), October 25, 1922.

"Naomi Eleanor Figaro." Find a Grave. Retrieved July 3, 2021. https:// www.findagrave.com/memorial/115017471/naomi-eleanor-figaro.

Nystrom, Justin A. "P. B. S. Pinchback." 64 Parishes. Retrieved May 9, 2022. https://64parishes.org/entry/p-b-s-pinchback.

Nystrom, Justin A. "White League." 64 Parishes. Retrieved July 12, 2021. https://64parishes.org/entry/white-league.

Peterson, Hannah Bethann. "Murder at Mer Rouge: A Dialogue on the Activities of the Ku Klux Klan in Northwestern Louisiana, 1921–1924." Senior Honors Thesis, Texas A&M University, 2004.

Pfeifer, Michael. "Lynching and Criminal Justice in South Louisiana." *Louisiana History* 40, no. 2 (1999): 155–77.

Potter, William Taylor. "Confederate monuments: Gen. Alfred Mouton led civil war against Lafayette's Black residents." *Daily Advertiser* (Lafayette, LA), July 30, 2020. Retrieved November 4, 2020. https://www.theadvertiser.com/in-depth/news/2020/07/30/confederate-monument-lafayette-controversial-general-alfred-mouton-organized-lynchings/5365029002/.

"Shadow of Ku Klux Klan Grows Larger in Congress and Nation." *New York Times*, December 10, 1922.

"Thibodaux Massacre." 64 Parishes. Retrieved on July 1, 2021. https://64parishes.org/entry/thibodaux-massacre.

"Thomas Fletcher Richards." Find A Grave. Retrieved July 8, 2020. https://www.findagrave.com/memorial/44249207/thomas-fletcher-richards.

"Troops on Duty Here as Trial of Negro Starts." *Daily Advertiser* (Lafayette, LA), October 23, 1922.

"Troops to Guard Negro Here Next Week, Indicated." *Daily Advertiser* (Lafayette, LA), October 21, 1922.

United Daughters of the Confederacy Alfred Mouton Chapter, Legal Documents 1870–1980, Box 1, File 6, Louisiana Room Collection, Edith Garland Dupré Library, University of Louisiana at Lafayette, Lafayette, LA.

Vincent, Charles. "Negro Legislators in Louisiana During Reconstruction." PhD diss. Louisiana State University, 1973.

Vincent, Charles, "Oscar Dunn." 64 Parishes. Retrieved May 9, 2022. https://64parishes.org/entry/oscar-dunn-2.

Watson, Melissa. "Civil rights history sheds light on area's racial past." *The Vermilion* (Lafayette, LA), September 20, 2017.

Printed in the USA
CPSIA information can be obtained
at www.ICGtesting.com
JSHW021046130923
48378JS00004B/122